God Is Good

Katie McCul
2 Timothy 3:16-17

Reflections on the

Book of Judges

Katie Erickson

WORLDVIEW WARRIORS
PUBLISHING

ISBN: 9798639328831

Table of Contents

Introduction

Judges 1

The book of Judges is one that you may not be familiar with. Perhaps you've read a few of the stories or heard about Samson and Delilah, but have you read through the whole book and studied each passage? When I was presented with the idea on writing through the book a section at a time, it definitely sounded intimidating, and I wondered if it would really be worthwhile.

On the other side of it, I can say that yes, it was a daunting venture to write through the whole book plus other topics that relate to it. But it was also very worthwhile to really dig into a Biblical book like this. But of all that books that could have been chosen, why should we study this big Old Testament book?

Before we get to that, it's important to define what a judge is in the context of this book. We think of a judge today as that person presiding over a courtroom, who listens to all the arguments and hands down a sentence on the accused. That is not what a judge is in the Biblical book of Judges. In this context, a judge is a military leader. A judge was to lead the people of Israel as they followed God's will for them and conquered the land promised to them. A judge of that day was more like a combination of president and military commander today than a courtroom-style judge.

A judge can also be seen as a type or model of Christ. Jesus Christ is our ultimate deliverer, rescuing us from death as the penalty we deserve for our sin. A judge was a temporary deliverer, sent to save the people from whatever enemy was before them. We can look at the judges and see Jesus Christ in their stories.

So, what's the deal with the book of Judges? It's the history of God's people, the people of Israel. I was never a big fan of history class in school, but I recognize that history is important to study. History is important to celebrate the victories that we have had as a people, but also if we don't know the mistakes that we have committed, then we're doomed to repeat them again. The book of Judges tells many stories of times that God's people were obedient to Him and were blessed for it, as well as many times when God's people were disobedient to Him and were cursed for it. These same principles still apply today, and we would be wise to take them to heart.

Context is extremely important when studying any Biblical book. Judges is a historical book that links the books of Joshua and 1 Samuel. It covers the time period from Joshua's day until the monarchy of Israel, when they first had a king. Judges also gives us the broader context for the book of Ruth, which happened during the same time period.

Under the rule of Joshua (who led the people after Moses), Israel had conquered and divided up the promised land. However, occupying the land wasn't so easy. In Judges, we see many battles that Israel engaged in to take over the land that God had given them. In Israel's case, the spiritual condition of the people (whether they were obeying or disobeying God) determined their political situation. When they followed God, He allowed them to conquer the other nations in their land and be delivered from oppression. When they turned against God and away from following Him, God would allow them to be oppressed by other nations.

With all that context understood, what happens in the first chapter of this book? The first thing they do in Judges 1:1-2 is to ask God to show them who should be in charge: "After the death of Joshua, the Israelites asked the Lord, 'Who of us is to go up first to fight against the Canaanites?' The Lord answered, 'Judah shall go up; I have given the land into their hands.'" Their leader Joshua had died, so they needed a new leader. The people of Judah being in charge was the first step in this process. The people of Israel here are those who had obeyed God and conquered the Promised Land.

I encourage you to go read the whole chapter of Judges 1, as it tells of a variety of successes and failures of the Israelite tribes in battles. In this section, we see the tribes addressed individually rather than the nation as a whole. There are many details given in this chapter, and they all show how Israel succeeded at times and failed at other times.

Just because Israel was God's chosen people didn't mean that they always had happy times. Similarly, being a follower of Jesus Christ today doesn't mean that your life will always be great and happy. Just as the people of Israel did, we all go through times where we do better or worse at following God's commands in our lives.

Join with me on this journey through the book of Judges, and I hope you find yourself in these stories.

Disobedience and Consequences
Judges 2:1-5

The angel of the Lord went up from Gilgal to Bokim and said, "I brought you up out of Egypt and led you into the land I swore to give to your ancestors. I said, 'I will never break my covenant with you, and you shall not make a covenant with the people of this land, but you shall break down their altars.' Yet you have disobeyed me. Why have you done this? And I have also said, 'I will not drive them out before you; they will become traps for you, and their gods will become snares to you.'" When the angel of the Lord had spoken these things to all the Israelites, the people wept aloud, and they called that place Bokim. There they offered sacrifices to the Lord.
~ Judges 2:1-5

Right before this passage, we see that Israel had experienced some great defeats (Judges 1:27-36). Here, the angel of the Lord is giving them the reason for those defeats: they disobeyed God. As it says in verse 2b, "Yet you have disobeyed me. Why have you done this?" God had delivered them from Egypt into the promised land of Canaan. God had made a covenant with the people that He will never break. Sounds like God did a lot of awesome stuff for them, right? So, you'd think they would be very grateful and thankful, right? Nope - instead, they disobeyed God's commands.

Because of their disobedience, they must receive a consequence. That consequence is that God will not help Israel drive out their enemies, and He will allow their enemies to trap them (verse 3). Any time that we disobey God, we too deserve to receive a negative consequence, according to God's natural law. Israel will reap what they sow, and so will we. We may not always see that consequence right away, but we will likely get one, unless God decides to show us His grace in that experience.

Are we happy when we get punished for doing something wrong? Not usually, and the people of Israel were no exception. In verses 4-5 we see that the people wept over this. They wept so much that they called that place Bokim, which literally means "weeping" in Hebrew. Their weeping doesn't necessarily mean that they were sorry for disobeying God, just that they did not like the negative consequence that was happening to them.

Negative consequences are one way that God encourages us to repent from our disobedience to Him. Repenting is not just feeling sorry for what you've done, but it's like turning around and walking the other direction, where you don't commit that sin anymore. If nothing bad ever happens when we sin, then we'd just keep on sinning, right? That's why God has to give consequences for our actions and allow us to reap what we sow. We as humans need to learn to obey God rather than to obey our sinful selves and disobey God. God is good, and we are sinful people. That is what the book of Judges is all about, and I think all of us today can definitely learn something from these stories we find in this book.

The Five Step Cycle
Judges 2:6-23

Grab your Bible and read Judges 2:6-23 before continuing on with this chapter.

This passage starts out with some of the historical context of this book. Joshua was the leader of the people of Israel after Moses, who brought them out of Egypt. Israel was faithful to God during the time of Joshua's leadership, so when he died, things changed. We see in Judges 2:10 that Joshua's generation did not leave a legacy of following God with the next generation. They were too far removed in time from the people who had left Egypt to have firsthand experience of God's deliverance then. If the people did not continue to share the importance and significance of that event, then the next generations were likely to go astray from God's purposes, and that's exactly what they did.

This story is the first one we see in Judges that sets up a pattern that is repeated often throughout the rest of the book. This repeated pattern has 5 steps to it:
1. Sin - The people disobey God.
2. Slavery - God allows them to be enslaved by their enemies.
3. Supplication - The people cry out to God for deliverance.
4. Salvation - God delivers them.
5. Silence - There is a time of peace.

We're going to take a look at this passage in light of these 5 steps, and we'll continue to use this structure in the coming chapters for other passages in Judges.

We see Israel's sin in verses 11-13: "Then the Israelites did evil in the eyes of the Lord and served the Baals. They forsook the Lord, the God of their ancestors, who had brought them out of Egypt. They followed and worshiped various gods of the peoples around them. They aroused the Lord's anger because they forsook him and served Baal and the Ashtoreths." Their sin was serving other gods instead of God Almighty. God had clearly laid this out as sin in Exodus 20:3-6.

We see Israel's slavery in verses 14-15: "In his anger against Israel the Lord gave them into the hands of raiders who plundered them. He sold them into the hands of their enemies all around, whom they were no longer able to resist. Whenever Israel went out to fight, the hand of the Lord was against them to defeat them, just as he had sworn to them. They were in great distress." Not only was Israel sold into the hands of their enemies, but God was against them any time they tried to fight their enemies. This was the negative consequence that they needed for their disobedience.

We see Israel's supplication in verse 15 ("Whenever Israel went out to fight, the hand of the Lord was against them to defeat them, just as he had sworn to them. They were in great distress.") and in verse 18b ("For the Lord relented because of their groaning under those who oppressed and afflicted them"). Israel did not like to be oppressed, and neither would we for that matter. They were in great distress; they cried out to God and groaned about their situation.

We see Israel's salvation in verse 16: "Then the Lord raised up judges, who saved them out of the hands of these raiders." God had a plan to bring them back from their disobedience and get them on the right track again. The problem was that they didn't stay in that salvation but instead continued to disobey God. Verses 17-19 say, "Yet they would not listen to their judges but prostituted themselves to other gods and worshiped them. They quickly turned from the ways of their ancestors, who had been obedient to the Lord's commands. Whenever the Lord raised up a judge for them, he was with the judge and saved them out of the hands of their enemies as long as the judge lived; for the Lord relented because of their groaning under those who oppressed and afflicted them. But when the judge died, the people returned to ways even more corrupt than those of their ancestors, following other gods and serving and worshiping them. They refused to give up their evil practices and stubborn ways."

We still see the period of silence in this passage, where God would deliver them and keep them safe from their enemies as long as the judge was alive, even though the people did not deserve it.

Have you had times in your life where you see yourself following this pattern? It may look a little different for you than being captured or oppressed by enemies, but you can probably see a similar cycle in your own life. Take some time to think about when you've gone through this, and perhaps where you're at on this cycle even now.

Othniel

Judges 3:7-11

The Israelites did evil in the eyes of the Lord; they forgot the Lord their God and served the Baals and the Asherahs. The anger of the Lord burned against Israel so that he sold them into the hands of Cushan-Rishathaim king of Aram Naharaim, to whom the Israelites were subject for eight years. But when they cried out to the Lord, he raised up for them a deliverer, Othniel son of Kenaz, Caleb's younger brother, who saved them. The Spirit of the Lord came on him, so that he became Israel's judge and went to war. The Lord gave Cushan-Rishathaim king of Aram into the hands of Othniel, who overpowered him. So the land had peace for forty years, until Othniel son of Kenaz died.
~ Judges 3:7-11

This passage starts out with a phrase that is common throughout the book of Judges: "The Israelites did evil in the eyes of the Lord" (Judges 3:7). We also saw this in the previous chapter (Judges 2:11) and we'll see it more throughout the book.

In the last chapter, I wrote about the 5-step cycle that happens often with the people of Israel throughout the book of Judges:
1. Sin - The people disobey God.
2. Slavery - God allows them to be enslaved by their enemies.
3. Supplication - The people cry out to God for deliverance.
4. Salvation - God delivers them.
5. Silence - There is a time of peace.

We see Israel's sin when they did evil and worshipped other gods, in verse 7: "The Israelites did evil in the eyes of the Lord; they forgot the Lord their God and served the Baals and the Asherahs." The Baals and Asherahs were pagan gods, so serving them was clearly forbidden by God back in Exodus 20:3-6.

Because of this sin, in verse 8 we read that God allowed them to be in slavery to the king of Aram Naharaim for 8 years. They needed to experience a negative consequence so that they would realize their sin and repent and turn away from it. We don't have any details on what this slavery entailed, but the general nature of slavery is that it's not a fun experience.

We see Israel's supplication and salvation in verses 9-10: "But when they cried out to the Lord, he raised up for them a deliverer, Othniel son of Kenaz, Caleb's younger brother, who saved them. The Spirit of the Lord came on him, so that he became Israel's judge and went to war. The Lord gave Cushan-Rishathaim king of Aram into the hands of Othniel, who overpowered him." Israel cried out to God, and God provided them Othniel as a deliverer, who saved them from the king's power.

We see silence for Israel in verse 11: "So the land had peace for forty years, until Othniel son of Kenaz died." They experienced peace until their deliverer died, and then the cycle starts all over again in the next passage.

How many times do we go through this same pattern in our lives? We're attracted to the allure of this world, so we sin and take our focus off of God and what he wants for us. One example of this is buying too many material possessions because we want them, when they're not things we truly need. This puts us in the slavery of being stuck in debt and spending too much money. Once we realize that we've messed up when we run out of money or see the mountain of debt continue to grow, we cry out to God and ask Him to help us get out of this mess! Hopefully at that point, we realize that it was us who messed it up and not put the blame on anyone else. In this case, our salvation comes through God helping us to realize what we should do and make better financial moves in life. This takes hard work, but focusing on God and His plan for us will get us through it so we may come out victorious on the other side. The time of silence comes when we ideally continue in the good pattern we've learned for many years to come.

This is just one example of how we can go through the same pattern as the people of Israel in the book of Judges. How do you see this happening in your life?

Eglon and Ehud
Judges 3:12-30

This passage of Judges 3:12-30 is a great story, so pull out your Bible and read it before continuing with this chapter.

Again, we see that "the Israelites did evil in the eyes of the Lord" (verse 12). We can look at this from our perspective and be amazed that they just didn't learn their lesson from what they've been through so far. But, if we take a good look at ourselves, we'll see that we really don't learn this lesson either!

Because of this continued sin, "The Israelites were subject to Eglon king of Moab for eighteen years" (verse 14). In the previous passage, they only had 8 years of slavery; now God has bumped that up to 18 years. Perhaps they need longer periods of slavery to get the point across that they shouldn't keep disobeying God.

Again, the people of Israel cried out to God, and God gave them a deliverer named Ehud (verse 15). The story of how Ehud killed Eglon, king of Moab, is a pretty interesting one, and perhaps not what you'd expect to read in the Bible! King Eglon was not a small man, in fact he was rather large. Ehud tells Eglon that he has a message from God for him, but instead of a verbal message, he whips out his sword and plunges it into the king's belly! King Eglon is so obese that the sword is completely swallowed up by his fat, even down to its handle. The passage tells us that his sword was about a cubit long, which is about 18 inches. Just picture that for a moment - an 18" sword being completely swallowed up by a man's fat! Yikes. Needless to say, Ehud left his sword there, and he fled the scene.

Nobody else was in the room at the time Ehud killed Eglon, so after a while, Eglon's servants started to get concerned. They honestly thought the king may be in the bathroom! After waiting "to the point of embarrassment" (verse 25), they finally unlocked the doors, went in, and saw the scene.

After Ehud delivered Israel from Eglon king of Moab, they experienced peace for 80 years. They had slightly longer slavery this cycle than last, but they also had twice as long of a period of peace as well.

While the story of Ehud killing Eglon is an entertaining one to us, it really does have a point, too. The people of Israel keep messing up and God gives them negative consequences for that, but He still continues to save them. But, He doesn't save them until they realize their mistakes.

The same is true for us. We need to realize what we're doing wrong, be truly sorry for it, turn away from our mistakes, and turn toward following God before He will save us. Do the people of Israel deserve God's salvation? Do we deserve God's salvation? No to both of those. But that's what God's grace is - a gift that we do not deserve.

It's important to note that as amazing as God's grace is, we don't have permission to keep sinning because of grace (see Romans 6:1-2). Our motivation needs to be such that we are truly trying to honor and obey God, not that we're sinning because we know we have a "get out of jail free" card. When we mess up and are truly sorry for it, God will always save us, just as He continued to do for the people of Israel throughout the book of Judges.

Deborah and Jael

Judges 4

Go read Judges 4 in your Bible, and then continue on reading this chapter.

With all of the gender issues that have been in the news and in our culture recently, it's interesting that gender can be perceived as a significant thing in this passage. One way to look at it is, "Wow - Israel had a female judge? That's pretty cool!" Another interpretation is, "Wow, Deborah was a great judge! Oh yeah, I guess she was female, too."

A lot of people turn the story of Deborah into one in which gender is the main focus, especially in today's culture where gender is often a hotly debated issue, whether it's the issue of women as pastors, a possible female president, transgender issues, or a variety of others. It's true that Deborah was the only recorded female judge of Israel, but her actions are significant regardless of her gender.

I must admit that I have a personal connection to the story of Deborah. I'm a woman working in the predominantly male field of engineering, and I also often serve in a pastoral role in various churches. I'm accustomed to being a female in a world of males. Not only that, but my parents actually named me Deborah when I was born. (Nobody ever really called me that, though, and I legally changed my name when I was 21 years old; but that's a long story.)

So, what's the story of Deborah all about? Deborah was a judge, and she followed the Lord in appointing a man named Barak to command 10,000 men in fighting this battle (verse 6). Barak, however, wouldn't go to battle without Deborah (verse 8)! This seems unusual, right - a man not wanting to be brave and courageous and go into battle without taking a woman? That shows the type of confidence and authority that Deborah had as the judge of Israel.

Deborah tells Barak that she'll go along, but because he wouldn't go without her, he won't receive the glory for the win. Verse 9 implies that Deborah will receive the glory instead, but stay tuned!

The enemy they were fighting against was a man named Sisera and his army. Sisera had a large army, complete with iron chariots, which definitely gave them an advantage over Israel. God was with Israel, so Sisera's entire army was slaughtered; verse 16 tells us that not a man was left! Sisera survived the battle and fled on foot. Sisera's family had an alliance with a family nearby, that of Heber the Kenite, so that's where he headed. And that's where we see the other woman in this story: Jael.

Jael was the wife of Heber the Kenite, and she met Sisera at her tent. She pretends to be protecting him, but then the tables are turned - she kills him with a tent peg! Barak comes by, and Jael shows him Sisera's dead body.

So, who got the glory? Barak's army won the battle, but Jael actually received the glory for killing Sisera, their opponent's commander.

Both Deborah and Jael are significant in this story, not just because they're female, but because they were obedient to what God wanted them to do, whether big things or small things. Deborah had the big job of being the leader over all of Israel, and she was obedient to God so Israel had God's favor in winning the battle. Jael ended up with a small job of killing Sisera, and she was obedient to God in that.

Regardless of your gender, how are you being obedient to God? Are you doing what He asks you to, even if it seems crazy? We, as followers of Christ, are all called to hear God's voice and obey it.

The Song of Deborah, Part 1
Judges 5:1-18

The victory that Israel experienced in Judges 4 against Sisera and his army was so significant that the people needed to remember it. If something like that happened today, it would be all over the media - newspapers, TV news reports, social media, Internet news sites, etc. Even things that aren't significant are often all over our media, but that's another topic for another day. A huge battle like this one deserved to be remembered, and they couldn't easily just write down all the details or prepare a news story and report on it from every angle like we could today. So, what did they do? They composed a song about it.

The chapter of Judges 5 is the song to remember the victory that Deborah and Barak had over Sisera. This poem is often called the "Song of Deborah." It is beautifully poetic, and it is a song of praise, thanksgiving, glory, and honor to God. It's not honoring those who fought in the battle, but it's honoring God, the true mastermind behind Israel's victory. It is believed that Deborah is the author of this poem, though we do not know that for certain. It is also believed that this was composed not too long after the events actually happened, so that they would be accurately remembered.

The poem starts out in verses 2-5 by giving praise to God. Verse 3 is especially significant: "Hear this, you kings! Listen, you rulers! I, even I, will sing to the Lord; I will praise the Lord, the God of Israel, in song." Think about that for a moment. Deborah, the judge and commander of Israel's army, just presided over this great victory. Assuming she is the one writing this, she is not at all praising herself. She is praising God completely for this victory! Now that's some serious humility there.

The song goes on in verses 6-8 with discussing the conditions of Israel at the time of battle. Things were not all that great. Canaanite robbers were present in their area, so trade and agriculture were threatened, and those were their way of life as a people.

Verses 9-11 go on to encourage the people to share of this victory. They need to keep remembering God's provision for them so that they don't turn away from Him again - even though we know that they will as we keep reading the book of Judges.

The final section we're looking at in this chapter is verses 12-18. These verses encourage all the tribes of Israel to work together to continue to go against their common enemy of the Canaanites. They are called to "Wake up!" which means they need to get up and take action rather than sit idly by.

The people of Israel recognized what God had done for them, and they wanted to make sure to remember this victory and give God the glory for it.

What has God done for you in your life? Are you giving Him the glory for it, and telling others about it to help honor God and remember what He has done? Or are you living your life thinking that you earned each little victory on your own? Think about it.

The Song of Deborah, Part 2
Judges 5:19-31

In the last chapter, we studied the first half of Judges 5, the song of Deborah to remember the battle that God won for her and Barak against Sisera and his armies. Here, we'll take a look at Judges 5:19-31, the rest of Deborah's song. The purpose of this song was to remember the battle and the victory that God gave them, and that is where we pick it up in this passage.

Verses 19-23 describe some more details of the battle itself. This section is clearly poetry, as there are literary devices such as repetition (words like "fought" and "river" appear multiple times) and imagery. Judges 4:12-16 previously described the battle in more detail, but this description is more poetic and fits the genre of a song. In verse 20 we see God beginning to intervene, with the personification of the stars. The enemy is described as getting swept away by the river, possibly reflecting back to God's victory over the Egyptian army at the Red Sea at the start of the exodus.

In the next section, verses 24-27, we see praise for Jael for her role in this battle. (For more context, go check out the chapter on Judges 4 to see what she did.) Jael is praised and blessed here for her actions, and that blessing is likely coming from the author rather than God Himself. The song here recounts how Jael treated Sisera well at first, until she lulled him into a false sense of security then killed him. In verse 27 we see again how poetic this passage is, with an instance of climactic parallelism, where the same actions are repeated for emphasis.

In verses 28-30, the scene shifts to one we did not see narrated in Judges 4: that of Sisera's mother. It can be easy for us to forget that all of these warriors and soldiers had family, too, and here there is compassion shown for Sisera's family by bringing up his mother waiting for her son to return home from battle. She longs for her son to return home, and that never happens.

Finally, in verse 31, we see the conclusion to this song about the battle. There is desire for more enemies to perish, and there is praise of God for giving them victory. We're reminded here that this battle brought 40 years of peace to Israel.

How many battles were fought, similar to the one recounted in Judges 4-5, for our freedom in the United States? How many people were courageous in their actions? How many mothers waited for their sons to return home from battle? All wars and battles bring devastation, but when they are fought as a part of God's plan, they ultimately bring peace. Because of this battle between Deborah, Barak, and Sisera, Israel had peace for 40 years. Because of the battles of the Revolutionary War in the 1770s, the United States gained independence as a nation. Many lost their lives in both battles, but God is still victorious.

May we, too, praise God for His provision and victory every day.

Who Are the Canaanites?

We have been going through the first few chapters of the book of Judges so far, but this is a good time to take a little break from that to go into a brief history of some of the people groups we see in Judges and elsewhere in the Bible. Context is important for interpreting any passage of the Bible, and part of the context is knowing the people and nations in that passage.

We read a lot in the Bible about the people of Israel as God's chosen people. But what about all the other people groups we read about? Where did they come from? Where are they today? For the next few chapters, I'll write on various Old Testament people groups, getting some of the content from the *Easton Dictionary of the Bible* and the *Holman Illustrated Bible Dictionary*. In this chapter, let's look at the Canaanites.

Where did the Canaanites come from? Well, we know that every person on earth at the time was wiped out by the Flood (Genesis 6:13), except for Noah and his three sons and all their wives. Noah's sons were Shem, Ham, and Japheth, and we see in Genesis 10:6 that Ham had a son named Canaan. If we continue reading Genesis 10:6-20, we see that the sons of Canaan became the Canaanites, and they scattered and took up a large geographic area.

A little bit later in history, we see Canaanites living near the sea and the Jordan River in Numbers 13:29. This was the Promised Land that God had promised to give to Israel, but Israel couldn't live there if the Canaanites were living there. We see in Exodus 23:23 that God will wipe out the Canaanites for them, and in Deuteronomy 20:16-17 God commands Israel to kill all of them, not leaving anything that breathes alive. Either way, Israel was supposed to take over the land of the Canaanites completely. The details of many of the battles that took place for this are in the book of Joshua.

The Canaanites did not worship the one true God. Even though they descended from Noah, somewhere along the line they developed their own pagan god, whom they named Baal. The name Baal is actually a Hebrew word meaning master or lord. We see a "showdown" between Baal and God with the prophet Elijah on Mt Carmel in 1 Kings 18, where Baal is clearly proven to be a false god.

So where are the Canaanites today? They were never fully wiped out by Israel, and they were later called the Phoenicians by the Greeks. The Canaanites / Phoenicians were famous as merchants, seamen, and artists, and they lived along the coastline of what is now Lebanon, Palestine, Israel, and Syria.

The next time you see something about Canaan in the Bible, you'll know a bit more about those people and who they were. This knowledge will hopefully help you have a better understanding of the Bible as a whole, which is important for growing in our faith and knowledge of God and His plan.

Who Are the Amalekites?

Who were the Amalekites, and where did they come from? It would be easy to assume that they're the descendants of Amalek (Genesis 36:12), but that's not the case. Amalek was the grandson of Esau, who was the grandson of Abraham. We see them in Genesis 14:7, which is during Abraham's time – four generations before Amalek was even born. However, we don't know exactly where the Amalekites descended from before this first mention.

The Amalekites were a nomadic tribe, meaning they didn't settle in one place but wandered the land as needed. They lived between the Dead Sea and the Red Sea, and it is believed that they migrated there from the Persian Gulf area.

The Amalekites often tried to stop Israel when Israel would be passing through their territory. We see a reference in Numbers 24:20 that the Amalekites were one of the first nations to attack the people of Israel after they left Egypt. Another battle with them is in Exodus 17:8-13. This is the battle where as long as Moses kept his hands up, Israel kept winning; if he lowered his hands, they started losing. Israel overcame the Amalekites in that battle, but they weren't fully wiped out. Later in Deuteronomy 25:17-19, we see God reminding Israel about how the Amalekites had attacked them and telling them that eventually they'll blot out that tribe.

This prophecy came true when the Amalekites were finally defeated once and for all by King Saul in 1 Samuel 14:48. Later, in 1 Samuel 30:18-20, King David recovered all of the Amalekites' treasures.

We don't know much more about the Amalekites, since they were completely wiped out. Very little archaeological evidence has been found from them because of their relatively short existence as a people. The Amalekites are one more nation that God used to either bless or curse Israel, depending on their obedience (or lack thereof) to Him.

Who Are the Amorites?

The Amorites were the descendants of one of the sons of Canaan (Genesis 10:15-18). We see them first mentioned in context in Genesis 14:7 where they were conquered, but not destroyed. In Genesis 14:13, we note that Abram (later known as Abraham) was an ally with Mamre, an Ammonite. Abram helped Mamre get his kingdom back, but later on the Amorites became enemies of Israel.

In Joshua 10:5-10 we read that the 5 kings of the Amorites were defeated by Joshua, and they were again defeated in Joshua 11 "until no survivors were left" (verse 8).

We read a little more about the Amorites in Judges 1:34-36. There we learn that they had trapped the weaker Israeli tribe of Dan, but then the tribes of Joseph (named for his sons Ephraim and Manasseh) were able to overpower them. In the time of Solomon in 1 Kings 9:20-21, we see that the Amorites were still around, and they were made to be slave labor to the Israelites.

Wait, the Amorites were all destroyed in Joshua 11, but then we're still hearing about them in Judges and 1 Kings, which came later chronologically? What's the deal with that? Well, the name Amorite is often used synonymously with the name Canaanite, and the Canaanites were a nation for a lot longer than these first Amorites we read about. It's like saying I'm an Ohioan and an American; both are correct, but one is a little more specific. There were lots of Canaanites, and the Amorites were one specific group of them, and somewhere in history the two names got mingled together and mixed up until they essentially meant the same people.

The Amorites occupied the land of Syria, including Palestine. They were warlike mountaineers. The Egyptians represented them in their hieroglyphics as people with fair skin, light hair, blue eyes, and pointed beards. The Amorites controlled the land of Babylon from 2000-1595 B.C. The most famous Amorite (who you still may not have heard of) was Hammurabi. Hammurabi wrote a code of laws, which was his version of how people should live. Hammurabi's code is sometimes compared with the Ten Commandments, since they are similar in nature of being ancient rules for living. However, the Ten Commandments were given by God, and Hammurabi was a regular man, though an important one in his day.

The Amorites are one example of how names can get confused over the course of history. Archaeologists and historians do their best to piece together who's who and what happened in history, and the Bible is a valuable resource in tracking some of these ancient nations.

Who Are the Midianites?

The Midianites are the descendants of Midian, who was the fourth son of Abraham by his lesser-known wife, Keturah (Genesis 25:1-2). The Midianites were an Arabian tribe who lived primarily in the northern deserts of Arabia. They were so dominant that they essentially ruled the Arabian Peninsula, even though their primary way of life was as shepherds. They were nomadic and did not settle in one particular location.

We first hear about the Midianites as a nation in Genesis 37:28, when Joseph was sold into slavery by his brothers to a Midianite caravan. The Midianites then sold Joseph to Potiphar in Egypt in Genesis 37:36. The next Biblical mention of them is generations later when Moses fled from Egypt to go to Midian (Exodus 2:15-21).

Because of this, the Midianites were generally friendly to the people of Israel right after their exodus from Egypt, as long as the Israelites stayed on the outlying part of the Midianites' lands. But when Israel started to get too far into the Midian lands, the Midianites joined forces with the Moabites to try and get rid of them before they took over. They convinced the Israelites to join in a festival to worship a pagan god, and Israel did. Naturally, God was not happy about this, so the Israelites were cursed. This resulted in a plague on Israel where more than 24,000 of the people died. (You can read the full story in Numbers 22-25.) But the Midianites did not go unpunished for this; their cities were conquered and burned, and five of their kings died (Joshua 13:21-22).

But that was not the end of the Midianites. Around 250 years later, they had regained their strength as a nation, and they joined with the Amalekites to wage war against Israel. But God raised up Gideon to fight them (Judges 6-7), and that was the end of the Midianites for good.

As you can see, God used the people of Midian in various ways in relation to His chosen people of the Israelites. They are both friend and foe at various times, and always used to further God's plan for His people and for the world.

How is God using the people around you in your life, even those who are different than you? Are you allowing God to use you to further His Kingdom in the lives of those around you?

Who Are the Philistines?

The most famous time we see the people of Israel interact with the Philistines is the story of David and Goliath, which you can read about in 1 Samuel 17. For those of you unfamiliar with the story, it's where young David has the courage to go up against the Philistines' giant Goliath in battle, and David easily defeats the giant with a slingshot, some stones, and the power of God, bringing victory to Israel.

But who were these Philistine people, and why were they Israel's enemies? They were a part of the primitive race of the Phoenicians. They lived in various parts of the Mediterranean, including in the valley of the Jordan River. We see in Exodus 13:17, Joshua 13:3, and 1 Samuel 4 that they inhabited the area between Judea and Egypt.

Throughout the Old Testament, it seems as though there's almost a continual war between the Philistines and the people of Israel, especially the southern tribes. Sometimes the Israelites were enslaved by the Philistines (Judges 15:11 and 1 Samuel 13:19-22) and other times Israel defeated them (1 Samuel 14). This war between the peoples did not stop until the reign of King Hezekiah (2 Kings 18:8), but they still occupied the land until they were ultimately defeated by the Romans.

Do you have a person in your life with whom it seems like you're constantly fighting? They just keep turning up where you don't want to see them and causing you grief. Maybe you had an incident that sparked the disagreement, or maybe it's just malice for a reason you can't explain. But for whatever reason, you just don't get along. That's the kind of relationship that the people of Israel had with the Philistines - they just didn't get along and were often fighting.

How did Israel handle the Philistines? That depended on the situation. At times, they followed God's leading and were victorious over them; at other times, they followed their own way of thinking and were beaten and enslaved.

How are you dealing with the difficult person (or people) in your life? Are you listening to God's leading in how to treat them, and therefore being victorious in having a better relationship with them? Or are you following your own way of thinking, and continuing to strain that already damaged relationship?

Use the example of Israel and the Philistines to take a look at difficult people you have in your life, and how God would want you to interact with them.

The Cycle Returns
Judges 6:1-10

The Israelites did evil in the eyes of the Lord, and for seven years he gave them into the hands of the Midianites. Because the power of Midian was so oppressive, the Israelites prepared shelters for themselves in mountain clefts, caves and strongholds. Whenever the Israelites planted their crops, the Midianites, Amalekites and other eastern peoples invaded the country. They camped on the land and ruined the crops all the way to Gaza and did not spare a living thing for Israel, neither sheep nor cattle nor donkeys. They came up with their livestock and their tents like swarms of locusts. It was impossible to count them or their camels; they invaded the land to ravage it. Midian so impoverished the Israelites that they cried out to the Lord for help.

When the Israelites cried out to the Lord because of Midian, he sent them a prophet, who said, "This is what the Lord, the God of Israel, says: I brought you up out of Egypt, out of the land of slavery. I rescued you from the hand of the Egyptians. And I delivered you from the hand of all your oppressors; I drove them out before you and gave you their land. I said to you, 'I am the Lord your God; do not worship the gods of the Amorites, in whose land you live.' But you have not listened to me."

~ Judges 6:1-10

Remember how earlier in the book of Judges we talked about the repeating pattern of sin, slavery, supplication, salvation, and silence? Well, it's back! After the 40 years of peace Israel experienced following their victory over Sisera's armies, Israel again falls into the trap of not following God.

In the first part of verse 1, we see Israel sinning again. We don't know details of that sin, but it's enough to say that they "did evil in the eyes of the Lord." The specific sin is relatively irrelevant, since all sin is evil in God's eyes and causes us to be separated from Him.

In the second part of verse 1, we see that Israel ended up in slavery to the Midianites because of their sin. But this wasn't any regular slavery; we see in verses 3-5 that both the Midianites and the Amalekites had invaded Israel's territory. They were killing Israel's crops and livestock, hoping to cause them to perish for lack of food and animals. This judgment that Israel received from the Midianites and the Amalekites was so bad that all they could do was hide in the hills.

What did Israel do to deserve this terrible treatment? Well for one thing, they did evil in the eyes of the Lord, so they deserved a punishment for that evil. But also, this curse was predicted back in Deuteronomy 28:31: "Your ox will be slaughtered before your eyes, but you will eat none of it. Your donkey will be forcibly taken from you and will not be returned. Your sheep will be given to your enemies, and no one will rescue them." This entire section of Deuteronomy 28 lets Israel know what will happen if they disobey God, and there's definitely a lot of bad stuff in there.

The pattern continues with Israel calling to God for help (supplication). We see in verse 6 that their situation got so bad that they finally decided to turn back to God. And when they did so, in verse 7, God sent them a prophet to help them out. The last time they cried out to God, He sent them Deborah and they were delivered. This time, however, God sends a prophet who doesn't immediately deliver them but instead shows them their sinful ways.

Who is this prophet? We really don't know, since not much description is given of him. But we do know that in verses 7-10, the prophet reminds Israel of how they have continually disobeyed God by worshiping the gods of the Amorites.

In this passage, we don't see Israel get to the point of being delivered and having silence or peace in the nation for a period of time. For now, they need to realize that their actions have consequences.

This passage brings to mind for me something that I was taught a number of years ago. I went to Christian schools, and I'll always remember some teachings that my high school freshman year religion teacher taught us. (Shout out to Mr. Gerlach at Lutheran High Westland!) He would often write on the board "O = B" and "D = C." What does that mean? It's really a shortened form of God's natural law. If we **O**bey God, we'll be **B**lessed (O = B). If we **D**isobey God, we'll be **C**ursed (D = C). That's how things worked for the Israelites back in the Old Testament, and that's how they work for us today as well.

We do have God's grace, especially after Jesus' death on the cross and resurrection, but God's natural law is still how the world works. O = B and D = C; if we obey God, we'll receive His blessing on our lives, but if we disobey God, we'll likely receive a curse. Which equation do you want to live by?

Gideon's Conversation

Judges 6:11-18

*The angel of the Lord came and sat down under the oak in Ophrah
that belonged to Joash the Abiezrite, where his son Gideon was
threshing wheat in a winepress to keep it from the Midianites. When
the angel of the Lord appeared to Gideon, he said, "The Lord is with
you, mighty warrior."*

*"Pardon me, my lord," Gideon replied, "but if the Lord is with us,
why has all this happened to us? Where are all his wonders that our
ancestors told us about when they said, 'Did not the Lord bring us
up out of Egypt?' But now the Lord has abandoned us and given us
into the hand of Midian."*

*The Lord turned to him and said, "Go in the strength you have and
save Israel out of Midian's hand. Am I not sending you?'*

*"Pardon me, my lord," Gideon replied, "but how can I save Israel?
My clan is the weakest in Manasseh, and I am the least in my
family."*

*The Lord answered, "I will be with you, and you will strike down all
the Midianites, leaving none alive."*

*Gideon replied, "If now I have found favor in your eyes, give me a
sign that it is really you talking to me. Please do not go away until I
come back and bring my offering and set it before you."*

And the Lord said, "I will wait until you return."

~ Judges 6:11-18

In this chapter, we move into the story of Gideon. You may have heard about Gideon before, but we're not quite to the "famous" part of his story yet.

In verse 11, we see that Gideon is just a regular guy doing his job when the angel comes to him. It was unusual though, because he was threshing in a winepress. Threshing is the process that separates the actual grains of wheat from the part of the stalk that isn't wanted, the chaff. Normally threshing would occur in a large open area, because the wind would assist in blowing away the lighter chaff, and the heavier grains of wheat would fall to the ground. Threshing in a winepress would be a lot more work, as more of it would need to be done manually.

So why was Gideon causing himself so much extra work? As we saw in the last chapter, it was because the Midianites were still oppressing the Israelites. By threshing in secret, Gideon was hoping to keep his crop for food rather than having it be taken away when the Midianites would see him. We see Gideon being timid by hiding his threshing, so it is especially ironic when he is called a mighty warrior by the angel in verse 12. This is a foreshadowing of what will happen in Gideon's future.

In verse 13, Gideon shares that he felt like the Lord had abandoned them because their present circumstances were so difficult. Is it God's fault that the people were in such a terrible predicament? Nope - it was Israel's fault for disobeying God. (Remember, disobeying God results in being cursed by Him rather than blessed.)

God does not address Gideon's complaint, however, and instead tells him in verse 14 to go fight for God. It's not about Gideon's power, but it's about his obedience to God and his willingness to trust God's strength. Gideon is not the only person who has thought he's too weak for the job that God is giving him; Moses acted similarly in Exodus 3, and so did Isaiah in Isaiah 6:8-9. Gideon's reluctance in verse 15 also resembles Moses's, but that is the point God is working on making here. God often uses the weak to accomplish His purposes. We see that echoed in the New Testament, in Paul's first letter to the Corinthians: "Brothers and sisters, think of what you were when you were called. Not many of you were wise by human standards; not many were influential; not many were of noble birth. But God chose the foolish things of the world to shame the wise; God chose the weak things of the world to shame the strong" (1 Corinthians 1:26-27).

As with Moses, God reassures Gideon that He really is sending him (verse 16). Again, like Moses, Gideon wants proof from God that it's really God sending Him on this mission, and God grants him that proof (verses 17-18).

Why does this encounter between Gideon and God matter for us today? We can be assured, like Gideon, that if God sends us on a mission, He will equip us to complete that mission. I've often said that if God brings me to it, God will bring me through it. Even if we're hiding away somewhere doing our threshing in a winepress, God will find us and use us if we're open to being obedient to Him. We need to be open to what God is leading us to, even if we feel as though we're not capable enough to accomplish it. Hear God's voice and obey it, and God will take care of the rest.

Who Is the Goddess Asherah?

We briefly interrupt our walk through the book of Judges to take a look at the goddess Asherah. Why? This goddess keeps coming up throughout the history of Israel, and you may be surprised at the fact that she is still worshipped today as well.

There are many references to Asherah and Asherah poles throughout the historical books of the Old Testament, including one coming up in Judges 6 that we'll address in the next chapter. Asherah is the name of a Canaanite goddess of sensuality and fertility. Asherah is believed to be the mother of 70 gods, of which Baal is the most well-known. The name Asherah was used to refer to both the goddess and the object of worship. Asherah's symbol was a tree without branches and her name can also be translated as "grove," which is why places of worship for Asherah were often a pole placed sticking out of the ground.

Asherah poles existed throughout Israel, both in the northern and southern kingdoms, when the people were straying from God and worshiping false gods. We see a number of times in the Old Testament that God commanded Israel to tear down all of the Asherah poles and stop worshipping her. At times they did, but she seemed to always creep back into their lifestyle when they allowed themselves to worship pagan gods. They even tried to brush it off as not being a big deal, as they often tried to incorporate worship of Asherah and other false gods into worship of the one true God.

They're worshiping the true God, so what would a little false god worship alongside that hurt, right?

One key fact for us to note here, which is true both for Israel and for us, is that we have the choice of who or what to worship in our lives. We can choose the one true God, or we can choose out of any number of pagan gods. It's always our choice. Do you choose to read your Bible, or do you choose to watch a sitcom on TV? Do you choose to pray and spend time hearing from God, or do you scroll through your social media feeds? Do you choose to meet with a church congregation to worship God together on Sunday morning, or do you sleep in? It's always a choice.

The gods we worship today do not necessarily have specific names like Asherah or Baal, nor do we often have shrines set up for them. But remember that Asherah was the goddess of sensuality and fertility. If you turn on your TV, what's the likelihood that you'll see something sensual on it? Pretty high, I'd say. Commercials, sitcoms, and even the nightly news seem to operate on the slogan that "sex sells." Everyone wants to sell you their product or get you to watch their show, and they use sex to do it. Huge million-dollar industries are built on the premise of sex and sensuality. Production and usage of Internet pornography is at an all-time high. Kids are being exposed to high amounts of nudity and sensuality at increasingly younger ages.

You may say that's just today's culture but remember that who or what we worship is a choice for every person. We have allowed ourselves and our culture to worship false gods, and doing so is dangerous. Once that door is opened, it is very hard to close it.

Have you opened that door in your life to allow false gods in? Is the goddess Asherah still around and being worshipped today? What do you think?

Gideon Meets God

Judges 6:19-27

Gideon went inside, prepared a young goat, and from an ephah of flour he made bread without yeast. Putting the meat in a basket and its broth in a pot, he brought them out and offered them to him under the oak.

The angel of God said to him, "Take the meat and the unleavened bread, place them on this rock, and pour out the broth." And Gideon did so. Then the angel of the Lord touched the meat and the unleavened bread with the tip of the staff that was in his hand. Fire flared from the rock, consuming the meat and the bread. And the angel of the Lord disappeared. When Gideon realized that it was the angel of the Lord, he exclaimed, "Alas, Sovereign Lord! I have seen the angel of the Lord face to face!"

But the Lord said to him, "Peace! Do not be afraid. You are not going to die."

So Gideon built an altar to the Lord there and called it The Lord Is Peace. To this day it stands in Ophrah of the Abiezrites.

That same night the Lord said to him, "Take the second bull from your father's herd, the one seven years old. Tear down your father's altar to Baal and cut down the Asherah pole beside it. Then build a proper kind of altar to the Lord your God on the top of this height. Using the wood of the Asherah pole that you cut down, offer the second bull as a burnt offering."

~ Judges 6:19-27

We started to hear Gideon's story two chapters ago, and here we'll pick it up again as Gideon and God continue their conversation.

God has told Gideon to do something crazy and outrageous, to save Israel from the Midianites who were badly oppressing them, and Gideon isn't so sure about that. He's not a strong guy, and he doesn't have a strong background. Gideon wanted a sign, so the angel provided one by sending fire and burning up Gideon's offering. The fire was a sign of acceptance of that offering.

But now, Gideon suspected that he would surely die, because he knew that he had seen the angel of the Lord. Seeing the actual face of God means certain death, and he knew that, so he was afraid, and with good reason. The angel reassures him, telling him to have peace. That command of having peace can be taken not just for Gideon as an individual, but as a foreshadowing that peace would come to their nation once again.

We then get to God's direct instructions to Gideon: tear down the altars to Baal and the Asherah poles. This was not a new thing, and any Israelite should have known better that they should only be worshipping the one true God. They had received similar commands previously in Exodus 32:12-13, Deuteronomy 7:5, and Judges 2:2, not to mention being told to not worship any other gods but Him in the Ten Commandments (Exodus 20:3-6).

Why was this a dangerous thing for Gideon to do? He was definitely going against mainstream society here. Baal worship was the popular thing to do, and everyone who was anyone worshipped Baal. The people also worshipped Asherah, the goddess of sexuality and fertility that we learned about in the last chapter, and they would be mad that the Asherah pole was torn down. Also, even though the Lord specified that this is Gideon's father's altar, it's not just their own family's personal place of worship. This altar and pole were used for their entire community, so it would be very obvious that they had been destroyed, and a lot of people would be mad. The instruction Gideon receives is to totally destroy the Asherah pole; once it was burned, it could not be re-used.

Naturally, as any of us would be, Gideon wasn't all gung-ho to go out and do this right away. But did he do it? We'll find out as we continue the story in the next chapter.

But first, why does this story matter to us today? We don't have any altars to Baal or any Asherah poles around. But even if the symbols of idol worship aren't as prominent in a physical way in our society, we still have idols and we all still worship them. It is important that we hear God's voice and listen to what He tells us is okay to do or not to do. Even if it goes against what's popular and seems right to society, we must always listen to God first. How are you doing that in your own life?

Gideon Tests God

Judges 6:28-40

*In the morning when the people of the town got up, there was Baal's
altar, demolished, with the Asherah pole beside it cut down and the
second bull sacrificed on the newly built altar!*
They asked each other, "Who did this?"
*When they carefully investigated, they were told, "Gideon son of
Joash did it."*
*The people of the town demanded of Joash, "Bring out your son. He
must die, because he has broken down Baal's altar and cut down the
Asherah pole beside it."*
*But Joash replied to the hostile crowd around him, "Are you going
to plead Baal's cause? Are you trying to save him? Whoever fights
for him shall be put to death by morning! If Baal really is a god, he
can defend himself when someone breaks down his altar." So
because Gideon broke down Baal's altar, they gave him the name
Jerub-Baal that day, saying, "Let Baal contend with him."*
*Now all the Midianites, Amalekites and other eastern peoples joined
forces and crossed over the Jordan and camped in the Valley of
Jezreel. Then the Spirit of the Lord came on Gideon, and he blew a
trumpet, summoning the Abiezrites to follow him. He sent
messengers throughout Manasseh, calling them to arms, and also
into Asher, Zebulun and Naphtali, so that they too went up to meet
them.*
*Gideon said to God, "If you will save Israel by my hand as you have
promised—look, I will place a wool fleece on the threshing floor. If
there is dew only on the fleece and all the ground is dry, then I will*

know that you will save Israel by my hand, as you said." And that is
what happened. Gideon rose early the next day; he squeezed the
fleece and wrung out the dew—a bowlful of water.
Then Gideon said to God, "Do not be angry with me. Let me make
just one more request. Allow me one more test with the fleece, but
this time make the fleece dry and let the ground be covered with
dew." That night God did so. Only the fleece was dry; all the ground
was covered with dew.
~ Judges 6:28-40

At the end of that passage we looked at in the previous chapter,
Gideon was commanded to tear down his community's altar to Baal
and the Asherah pole. This was a pretty big deal, because Gideon
was sure the people would get mad at him for it - and at the start of
this passage, we see that's exactly what happened. Gideon had taken
away what they considered to be sacred.

The people were mad at Joash, Gideon's father, since Joash was the
one responsible for the town's Baal altar and Asherah pole. After
their investigation and discovering that Gideon had torn down their
"sacred" places, they asked Joash to get Gideon so they could
properly punish him. But it's interesting in verse 31 that even Joash
doesn't fully believe in Baal as a God. Notice how he says "IF Baal
really is a god…" Even though Joash apparently doubted Baal's
status as a god, that didn't stop him from being tolerant and having
the altar anyway.

Fortunately, because of his dad's help, Gideon does not receive the
death penalty, but he does get a new nickname - Jerub-Baal. This
was supposed to be a derogatory name meant to show the
punishment that the people thought Gideon would face. But instead,
it became a good reminder of God's victory over Baal, and how God
is the only one who should be worshipped.

The bigger picture here is what had happened to Israel as a people.
Back in Deuteronomy 13:6-10, Moses commanded that even close
relatives be stoned for idolatry. Obviously, idolatry was a pretty big
deal, with it being deserving of death as a punishment! Yet, here was
not just one or two people but an entire town practicing it very

publicly. The people had started to believe the lies of the surrounding peoples and they had started worshipping their gods. The lies had crept in and become "truth" to the people of Israel, so much so that they no longer saw it as sin. They believed they could worship Baal and Asherah right along with God. Instead of putting someone to death for worshipping a god other than the one true God, the people were ready to put Gideon to death for not worshipping their gods!

All this local-level drama about the false god worship was then eclipsed by an invasion of the Midianites. Israel wasn't going to go down without a fight, so Gideon gathered the troops. Verse 34 says how Gideon summoned the Abiezrites. They were like Gideon's clan, his tribe, or very extended family so to speak. For extra reinforcement, he also called in the Israelite tribes of Manasseh, Asher, Zebulun, and Naphtali. But even with all that, Gideon lacked faith and confidence in God's promises. He needed multiple signs of reassurance. That's where the fleece comes in; Gideon tests God not once but twice to make sure that His promises are true. Both times God comes through and assures Gideon that He will take care of them, as promised.

Gideon appears to make arbitrary demands on God, simply to receive a sign. This is not necessarily recommended for Christ followers today, as it can be seen as testing God (which is forbidden in Deuteronomy 6:16 and reaffirmed by Jesus in Matthew 4:7, by the way). What we should do is to carefully observe what God is doing in our circumstances, pray, and read His Word to have the assurance and confidence that we need.

But in spite of Gideon's apparent lack of faith, God still chose to prove himself to Gideon and to use him for His purposes. How are you doing with that? Are you allowing God to speak into your life and use you for whatever He needs to accomplish in His Kingdom? Or are you mad because someone tore down your "altars" and the things that distract you from God?

What Are the Odds?
Judges 7:1-8

Early in the morning, Jerub-Baal (that is, Gideon) and all his men camped at the spring of Harod. The camp of Midian was north of them in the valley near the hill of Moreh. The Lord said to Gideon, "You have too many men. I cannot deliver Midian into their hands, or Israel would boast against me, 'My own strength has saved me.' Now announce to the army, 'Anyone who trembles with fear may turn back and leave Mount Gilead.'" So twenty-two thousand men left, while ten thousand remained.

But the Lord said to Gideon, "There are still too many men. Take them down to the water, and I will thin them out for you there. If I say, 'This one shall go with you,' he shall go; but if I say, 'This one shall not go with you,' he shall not go."

So Gideon took the men down to the water. There the Lord told him, "Separate those who lap the water with their tongues as a dog laps from those who kneel down to drink." Three hundred of them drank from cupped hands, lapping like dogs. All the rest got down on their knees to drink.

The Lord said to Gideon, "With the three hundred men that lapped I will save you and give the Midianites into your hands. Let all the others go home." So Gideon sent the rest of the Israelites home but kept the three hundred, who took over the provisions and trumpets of the others.

Now the camp of Midian lay below him in the valley.
~Judges 7:1-8

Just before this, Gideon had tested God and was now confident that God would give them victory over Midian. But now we see how that actually plays out.

Gideon's army was already outnumbered 4:1 by the Midianite army. The numbers were against them, but Gideon had confidence in God that he would take care of them. Things looked a little improbable, but God can handle 4:1 odds, right? So when God tells Gideon that he has too many men, that had to be quite a surprise to Gideon! But even with 4:1 odds against him, having a large army could cause Israel to take credit for their win, rather than giving the glory to God.

The elimination round was to essentially let the cowards go home. This was not a new or unusual thing for Israel, in fact we see it referenced in Deuteronomy 20:8. The idea behind it was that fear spreads easily. If some of the men were afraid, that fear could become contagious and more and more men would become too afraid to fight, thus limiting the army's power and courage. This sent 22,000 men back home - more than 2/3 of the army! If the odds were slim before, now they're even worse – more like 13:1.

But leaving Gideon with just 10,000 men (against around 128,000 men for the Midianites) was still too many in God's eyes, so they moved on to the second elimination round. If a man drank from the river with his cupped hands, he stayed; if not, he went home. That eliminated another 9,700 men - Gideon's army was now down to only 300 men! The odds were definitely not in their favor, at over 426:1.

The way the men drank water seems like an odd factor for their qualification to fight in the army, but we can't always understand God's ways. God knew what He was doing with this, and Gideon had to trust that. Gideon had to trust that God was still going to use the situation for his glory, even though it seemed like a total long shot and nearly impossible from a human perspective.

Previously, Gideon had tested God a number of times to make sure he could trust Him. Now, the tables were turned, and God was testing Gideon's faith. Going up against the huge Midianite army with his now itty-bitty army seemed crazy, but Gideon knew that this was what God wanted him to do, so he was obedient in moving forward with that.

Has God ever asked you to do something that seemed strange at the time? How did He later use that situation for His glory? If you haven't seen that part of it yet, perhaps it's still on the horizon. The important thing is that when God tells us to do something, however strange it sounds, we must trust God and obey, so we can give Him the glory when it all works out according to God's plan in the future.

Preparing for Victory
Judges 7:9-18

*During that night the Lord said to Gideon, "Get up, go down against
the camp, because I am going to give it into your hands. If you are
afraid to attack, go down to the camp with your servant Purah and
listen to what they are saying. Afterward, you will be encouraged to
attack the camp." So he and Purah his servant went down to the
outposts of the camp. The Midianites, the Amalekites and all the
other eastern peoples had settled in the valley, thick as locusts. Their
camels could no more be counted than the sand on the seashore.
Gideon arrived just as a man was telling a friend his dream. "I had
a dream," he was saying. "A round loaf of barley bread came
tumbling into the Midianite camp. It struck the tent with such force
that the tent overturned and collapsed."*

*His friend responded, "This can be nothing other than the sword of
Gideon son of Joash, the Israelite. God has given the Midianites and
the whole camp into his hands."*

*When Gideon heard the dream and its interpretation, he bowed
down and worshiped. He returned to the camp of Israel and called
out, "Get up! The Lord has given the Midianite camp into your
hands." Dividing the three hundred men into three companies, he
placed trumpets and empty jars in the hands of all of them, with
torches inside.*

*"Watch me," he told them. "Follow my lead. When I get to the edge
of the camp, do exactly as I do. When I and all who are with me blow
our trumpets, then from all around the camp blow yours and shout,
'For the Lord and for Gideon.'" ~Judges 7:9-18*

Naturally, Gideon was afraid going into this battle. He had less than 1% of his original army left, and the odds were definitely not in his favor. His army of just 300 men was up against around 128,000 Midianites. God had a plan, however, and the huge difference in the size of the armies was to show His glory. Gideon was getting discouraged and desired another sign from God, so that he could be convinced that God really would make them victorious over the Midianites.

God gives Gideon a sign in the form of a dream, but not his own dream. In that culture, dreams were considered an important means of communication from the divine. Think back to Joseph (of the "coat of many colors" fame) and the dreams he had, foreshadowing how God would bless him by making his brothers and father bow down to him (Genesis 37:1-11), for example.

After sneaking into the enemy camp at God's insistence, Gideon overhears one of the Midianites telling another about a dream he had. In that dream, it was clear even to the Midianites that God was going to make Israel victorious over them.

This eavesdropping was entirely not coincidence, so that was exactly the sign that Gideon needed. He worshipped God, then got Israel ready for a sneak attack battle.

The trumpets used in battle were more for making noise and signaling to other parts of the army than for playing music. Normally only the leaders would have trumpets, so having 300 of them (one for each man) in this case made it sound like they were a much larger army than they were. That was part of the plan to surprise and confuse Midian's army.

Gideon's instructions to his army probably sounded weird to them. After all, who could win a battle simply by blowing trumpets and yelling? (Apparently, they had forgotten about the battle of Jericho back in Joshua 6.) This sounded like a strange way to win a battle, but Gideon and his army needed to have confidence in God's plan, as weird as it may sound to them. They knew that without God's power, their puny army didn't stand a chance against Midian's large army.

Size doesn't matter when you're dealing with God's plan. The little guy can win over the giant with God's help (think David and Goliath). Do you feel weak, powerless, and insignificant? That's the best time to have trust in God and let Him use you and your life to fulfill His purposes. How are you letting God use you?

Surprise!

Judges 7:19-25

Gideon and the hundred men with him reached the edge of the camp at the beginning of the middle watch, just after they had changed the guard. They blew their trumpets and broke the jars that were in their hands. The three companies blew the trumpets and smashed the jars. Grasping the torches in their left hands and holding in their right hands the trumpets they were to blow, they shouted, "A sword for the Lord and for Gideon!" While each man held his position around the camp, all the Midianites ran, crying out as they fled.

When the three hundred trumpets sounded, the Lord caused the men throughout the camp to turn on each other with their swords. The army fled to Beth Shittah toward Zererah as far as the border of Abel Meholah near Tabbath. Israelites from Naphtali, Asher and all Manasseh were called out, and they pursued the Midianites. Gideon sent messengers throughout the hill country of Ephraim, saying, "Come down against the Midianites and seize the waters of the Jordan ahead of them as far as Beth Barah."

So all the men of Ephraim were called out and they seized the waters of the Jordan as far as Beth Barah. They also captured two of the Midianite leaders, Oreb and Zeeb. They killed Oreb at the rock of Oreb, and Zeeb at the winepress of Zeeb. They pursued the Midianites and brought the heads of Oreb and Zeeb to Gideon, who was by the Jordan.

~Judges 7:19-25

Gideon had just given his army the instructions to blow their trumpets and shout as their plan of attack, so that's exactly what they did. The primary weapons they were using were noise and confusion - trumpets, the sudden light of the torches, and their battle cry. Seems like that wouldn't be too effective, right? Especially when they were outnumbered well over 400 to 1. But with God on their side, the odds didn't matter.

The Midianites were surprised and confused. They were suddenly afraid of this supposedly large army, and they panicked. They got confused and thought their enemies were already among them, so they started fighting against themselves and killing one another! The Israelites didn't have to kill the Midianites; the Midianites took care of that for them.

What was left of the Midianite army fled away, so Gideon enlisted help from another Israelite tribe, Ephraim. His own army had gotten their courage back after seeing what God had done for them, so they pursued Midian as well.

There was no way this battle would have had the victorious outcome that it did except through God's providence. Think about how silly this would look, to have a huge army turn on itself simply because you surprised them and were loud! This makes no sense to human ways of thinking, but that is exactly the point.

If Israel had won the battle on her own strength, Israel would have gotten the glory. Because the battle was won in such a unique and improbable way, God gets the glory.

What's going on in your life that seems like a long shot? If it's truly of God, you will be victorious if you're obedient to what God is telling you, just like Gideon was.

God's Victorious Power
Judges 8:1-21

Grab your Bible to read this passage of Judges 8:1-21 before continuing on. As we saw in the last chapter, Gideon's small army fights against the large Midianite army. Midian ran away, so Gideon is pursuing them with the help of the tribe of Ephraim.

Gideon, still leading his small army, requests food for his troops from the people of Sukkoth. Sukkoth was part of the land given to the tribe of Gad, which was part of Israel, so they were all on the same side. You'd think the town of Sukkoth would be willing to help their brothers, but that was not the case. They feared that if the people of Midian (their enemies) found out that they had helped Gideon, Midian would punish them for it. They were geographically close to the site of the battle, so they feared that Midian would regroup, come back, and try to fight them.

So, Gideon moves on to Peniel, another nearby town, and makes the same request. The same thing happens again! Gideon then threatens both of these towns with punishment when he goes on to apprehend the kings of Midian, even without their help.

Gideon goes on to meet up with the much larger army of Midian. Midian is again surprised by this; after all, what little tiny kid goes chasing after the huge bully? Midian thought they were far enough away that they wouldn't be pursued, but they thought wrong. Gideon captured the two kings of Midian, therefore disbanding their army and officially winning the battle.

After this victory, which was again due to God's power, Gideon remains true to his word. He went back to the towns of Sukkoth and Penial to punish their leaders, and then he killed the kings of Midian.

We see here yet again that it was only through God's power that Gideon's small army of 300 was victorious. God was with them, and Gideon had faith and confidence in what God would do. Gideon was called by God and was obedient to Him, so He knew God would bless him for that. It was incredibly improbable that Gideon's tiny army would defeat Midian's huge one, but it was because of the faith of their leader, Gideon, that they even attempted such a feat. Gideon needed signs and reassurances along the way, but he kept the faith and was victorious in the end because of following God's leading in his life.

Gideon even had opposition from his own people when he asked for help and they turned him down, but he pressed on anyway. Gideon was more concerned with what God was telling him than what the world was telling him.

How often can you say that in your own life? It's very easy for us to listen to God when He seems to be agreeing with what the world is telling us. But it's much more difficult to listen to God when that goes against the world's ideals, and even more difficult when following God could very easily lead to our personal harm.

So how do we be obedient to God, even when the world is telling us not to? Remain strong in your faith. Build up your relationship with God through prayer and reading His Word. Listen to what God is telling you, and like Gideon, have the faith and trust to go for it.

Gideon's Reward

Judges 8:22-28

The Israelites said to Gideon, "Rule over us—you, your son and your grandson—because you have saved us from the hand of Midian."
But Gideon told them, "I will not rule over you, nor will my son rule over you. The Lord will rule over you." And he said, "I do have one request, that each of you give me an earring from your share of the plunder." (It was the custom of the Ishmaelites to wear gold earrings.)
They answered, "We'll be glad to give them." So they spread out a garment, and each of them threw a ring from his plunder onto it. The weight of the gold rings he asked for came to seventeen hundred shekels, not counting the ornaments, the pendants and the purple garments worn by the kings of Midian or the chains that were on their camels' necks. Gideon made the gold into an ephod, which he placed in Ophrah, his town. All Israel prostituted themselves by worshiping it there, and it became a snare to Gideon and his family. Thus Midian was subdued before the Israelites and did not raise its head again. During Gideon's lifetime, the land had peace forty years.
~ Judges 8:22-28

We've been reading about Gideon and his small army battling the Midianites. We read how God made it clear that He would get the glory for the victory, not Gideon, because the Midianite army was over 400 times larger than Gideon's. Then we read how even after

Gideon's army made the Midianites retreat, they chased them and apprehended their kings.

Now, after all that, Gideon returns home as a triumphant leader. The people of Israel, knowing of Gideon's great victory, want to make him their leader. They want to worship Gideon as being victorious, rather than worshipping God. Fortunately, Gideon is humble and realizes this, and he puts a stop to it.

Gideon does, however, take a reward for his victory. He requests gold earrings from the people, which he makes into an ephod. I'm sure that's just what anyone today would want, right? "Gideon, you've just won a huge victory over the Midianites, what are you going to do now?" "I'm making an ephod!"

So what exactly is an ephod? Take a look at the next chapter for a more detailed description, but the short version is it's a fancy apron-like garment.

It's important to note that the gold for the ephod actually came from the Midianites. In verse 24 we see that it came from the "plunder," which was the items they took from the Midianites when they fled. Gideon wasn't asking for the Israelites to give up their possessions, but rather a small part of what they received because of his obedience to God that resulted in Israel's victory.

But the ephod was also associated with idol worship in that day. Remember how back in Judges 6, Gideon destroyed the people's altar to Baal and their Asherah pole? It really wasn't that long ago that the people were worshipping those idols. The people yearned to have a physical object to worship, rather than only worshipping the one true God. Old habits are hard to break, so the people began to worship Gideon's ephod.

Even though the people were still not worshipping only the one true God, they still had peace from the Midianites for 40 years.

What can we learn from this? The main lesson for us today is that we need to worship God, not other people or man-made objects. While

I'm guessing you don't have a gold ephod that you worship, we do have many other things in our lives that we treat as idols over God. We worship sports teams, musicians, movie stars, or even put our families and friends as more important than God in our lives. We often worship whatever makes us feel good, which is not necessarily God and can often be things that are sinful.

Follow Gideon's example and worship God with your entire life, giving Him all of the glory for everything He has done for you.

What Is an Ephod?

We read in the last chapter that Gideon received an ephod from the people for his victory over the Midianites.

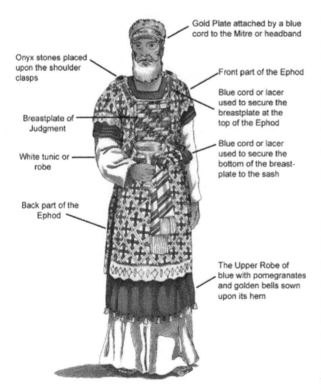

Onyx stones placed upon the shoulder clasps

Breastplate of Judgment

White tunic or robe

Back part of the Ephod

Gold Plate attached by a blue cord to the Mitre or headband

Front part of the Ephod

Blue cord or lacer used to secure the breastplate at the top of the Ephod

Blue cord or lacer used to secure the bottom of the breastplate to the sash

The Upper Robe of blue with pomegranates and golden bells sown upon its hem

What does an ephod look like? This picture is an example that points out the different parts of a high priest's outfit, which includes the ephod.

The ephod was often made of fine linen. It had two pieces (a front and a back) joined together over the shoulders. It was worn on top of the tunic. The high priest's ephod would be embroidered with many colors, while others would be much simpler.

So, the ephod was a sacred vestment, which is like article of clothing. It was originally worn by the high priest (Exodus 28:4) but later was worn by regular priests (1 Samuel 22:18). We also see Samuel wearing an ephod in 1 Samuel 2:18, and David wearing one in 2 Samuel 6:14.

So far it sounds like an ephod is a good thing, used for worshiping God, right? Well, there's another definition of that same word that isn't so good. The word ephod is also associated with idol worship. In Gideon's story, the people began to worship Gideon's ephod rather than God, and that is clearly idolatry. This also happened in the book of Hosea, as referenced in Hosea 3:4.

Scholars believe that it started out that the ephod was worn to worship God, then it was worn to worship foreign gods (idols), then the people would put the ephod on the idol statue, and the term then became synonymous with idol worship.

So, are ephods important today? If you're talking about the garment itself, then not really. Ephods are not generally worn or seen anywhere today, except possibly for some Jewish religious ceremonies. But the idea behind it is definitely still important. Idol worship is still a bad idea and goes against how God created us - to worship Him and Him alone. Anything that we worship, whether it's a statue, a person, or a piece of clothing, is wrong and is disobedient to God.

While the details of the physical garment of an ephod are not very relevant today, perhaps thinking of it will help you remember to keep your heart pure and not worship anything except the one true God.

Life After Gideon
Judges 8:29-35

Jerub-Baal son of Joash went back home to live. He had seventy sons of his own, for he had many wives. His concubine, who lived in Shechem, also bore him a son, whom he named Abimelech. Gideon son of Joash died at a good old age and was buried in the tomb of his father Joash in Ophrah of the Abiezrites.
No sooner had Gideon died than the Israelites again prostituted themselves to the Baals. They set up Baal-Berith as their god and did not remember the Lord their God, who had rescued them from the hands of all their enemies on every side. They also failed to show any loyalty to the family of Jerub-Baal (that is, Gideon) in spite of all the good things he had done for them.
~Judges 8:29-35

We're finally coming to the end of Gideon's story. After his victory in battle, thanks to his obedience to God, followed by the people wanting to honor him for that, Gideon settles back into life at home. His many wives and sons indicate his prosperity in that day. God honored Gideon's obedience to Him by giving him a large family.

One of Gideon's concubines is singled out in this passage. A concubine is similar to a wife, but with lower status; another word for one could be a mistress. It should be noted that just because Gideon had many wives and concubines doesn't make it ok in God's eyes. Gideon was still a human, prone to sinful tendencies, and this was one of them.

This one particular concubine of Gideon's lived in the town of Shechem. She was still under her father's household and authority, but Gideon would visit her periodically. (Again, just because Gideon did it does not make this ok in God's eyes!) She is singled out because she bore Gideon a son named Abimelech, who we'll read about more as we continue through Judges.

The fact that verse 32 says that Gideon died "at a good old age" indicates that he had a long and full life. This expression is used elsewhere in the Old Testament to describe Abraham (Genesis 25:8) and David (1 Chronicles 29:28).

What happened after Gideon died? The people began to worship idols again (verse 33). The phrase "When the cat's away, the mice will play" comes to mind here. Gideon was the one who had destroyed their altars to Baal and their Asherah poles, so once he was gone, they essentially built them right back up again. They began to worship the false god Baal-Berith; this literally means "lord of the covenant." This was their blatant disregard for the covenant that Israel had with God, which they were now clearly abandoning, yet again.

Israel continued to forget God's provision for them, and they constantly turned to the things of this world. God had rescued them in a triumphant victory from the horrible oppression of the Midianites, and now they completely turned their backs on Him!

But how often do we do that as well? Maybe the power of God set you free from an addiction, and then you soon get addicted to something else. Maybe you briefly praise God for something good that He did in your life, but the next day you turn your back on God and rely on yourself again. We do this all the time, because we're a sinful people, but that's no excuse. We need to try to be more like Gideon and less like the Israelites, turning to God and relying on Him rather than following other people or the ways of this world. People come and go, but we are continually called to follow the one true God.

Meet Abimelech

Judges 9:1-21

The story in this passage of Judges 9:1-21 revolves around
Abimelech, who was one of Gideon's 70 sons from his various
wives and concubines. Abimelech was born of a concubine (who is
lesser status than a wife) who still lived under her father's household
in Shechem. Interestingly, Abimelech's name literally means "my
father is king" (in Hebrew, "ab" means father, the "i" means my, and
"melech" means king). Gideon was not the king, although the people
wanted him to be after his victory over the Midianites. Perhaps
Abimelech's mother the concubine wanted to honor Gideon by
naming their son Abimelech; we don't have that detail recorded in
Scripture.

Abimelech had 69 half-brothers, and he was likely shunned by many
of them because his mother was a lowly concubine, not even a full-
fledged wife. He appeals to his brothers to get more prestige and
recognition from them. Abimelech makes the logical argument that
it'd be better for one man to rule over the people instead of 70. I've
been involved in projects with multiple leaders, and I can agree that
such a situation never works out well. Abimelech appeals to the
people of Shechem to make him their leader. The city of Shechem
was on an important trade route, so it was a prominent city in the
region. It was founded by the Canaanites, and it's likely that the
people maintained a link with them.

Abimelech is worried that the people will choose another of his brothers instead of him, so he gets rid of the competition. He hires people to kill all of his half-brothers except for the youngest, Jotham. The people of Shechem apparently don't care that Abimelech is essentially a murderer, so they make him their king!

Jotham knows Abimelech's true character, so he's compelled to warn the people about the person they just put in charge. He uses a fable to explain Abimelech's true character. This is the same literary technique that Jesus uses with His parables in the Gospels.

In Jotham's fable (Judges 9:8-15), he uses the imagery of trees and plants. First the trees want the olive tree to be king. It was a very valuable tree, with its oil being used for lamps and its olives for food and medicine. But the olive tree had important functions, so it declined to be king. Next the fig tree was nominated. Figs were a key crop, however, so it too declined. Third, the grape vine was suggested. But its vines are good for wine, so the vine also declines being king. Finally, there's the thorn bush. It's really not good for anything, so since it's not doing anything, it might as well be king, right?

Even though Jotham's point seems pretty clear, in Judges 9:16-20 he provides an explanation. Gideon was the olive tree, and Abimelech is the thorn bush. It's not wise to make someone your king just because they have the time and motivation to do it; they should really be a qualified leader. But since the people seemed to like Abimelech, Jotham fled the area after calling them out.

So how does this apply to us? Here in the United States, every four years the election drama heats up and we prepare to choose a new leader for our country. Who is an olive tree? Who is a thorn bush? With any political decision, take a look at the candidates and pray about who God would have to lead in that role.

This also applies in the non-political realms of our lives. Everyone is a leader in some way, whether you have an official leadership title and position or not. You may be a leader in your household. You may be a leader for your friends at school. You may be a leader to a younger sibling. We are all leading someone, so what kind of leader are you? Are you cruel and ruthless like Abimelech, or are you following God's ways and imitating Him in your leadership?

Examine your life and the leaders in it, and pray to God to help you make wise choices.

Abimelech's Leadership

Judges 9:22-29

*After Abimelech had governed Israel three years, God stirred up
animosity between Abimelech and the citizens of Shechem so that
they acted treacherously against Abimelech. God did this in order
that the crime against Jerub-Baal's seventy sons, the shedding of
their blood, might be avenged on their brother Abimelech and on the
citizens of Shechem, who had helped him murder his brothers. In
opposition to him these citizens of Shechem set men on the hilltops to
ambush and rob everyone who passed by, and this was reported to
Abimelech.*
*Now Gaal son of Ebed moved with his clan into Shechem, and its
citizens put their confidence in him. After they had gone out into the
fields and gathered the grapes and trodden them, they held a festival
in the temple of their god. While they were eating and drinking, they
cursed Abimelech. Then Gaal son of Ebed said, "Who is Abimelech,
and why should we Shechemites be subject to him? Isn't he Jerub-
Baal's son, and isn't Zebul his deputy? Serve the family of Hamor,
Shechem's father! Why should we serve Abimelech? If only this
people were under my command! Then I would get rid of him. I
would say to Abimelech, 'Call out your whole army!'"*
~ Judges 9:22-29

In the last chapter, we saw how Gideon's son Abimelech came into
power as the leader of the tribe of Manasseh. Jotham, the only
remaining one of Abimelech's 69 half-brothers, warned the people

that they're not choosing the right man to lead them, but they didn't listen.

Manasseh was one of the smaller and weaker tribes of Israel, but being their leader still gave Abimelech a power trip. He wasn't exactly what you'd call everyone's favorite leader; he was more like a tyrant or a dictator instead of being a judge with the people's best interests at heart as previous rulers had been.

Shechem, the setting of this section of Judges, was one of the main towns in Manasseh, and it was along a primary trade route for the area. The people there did not get along well with Abimelech. The citizens of Shechem fought back when Abimelech's men basically sabotaged the economy. They would rob the traders who came there, which caused the economy to crash, because people were afraid to come through there, lest they get robbed as well. Even though Abimelech did not live there and had appointed a man named Zebul to rule directly in Shechem, this would still hurt the area of which Abimelech was in charge.

Meanwhile, a man named Gaal moves into town. Gaal was a Canaanite, and he was very opposed to having an Israelite such as Abimelech ruling over the area of Manasseh. Gaal questions Abimelech's qualifications to be their ruler. Abimelech's mother was from Shechem, though we do not know if she was Canaanite, Israelite, or from another people group, and his father Gideon was clearly an Israelite.

During the harvest festival that honored the false god Baal-Berith, Gaal starts stirring up trouble for Abimelech. Gaal claimed that he would be a better leader for the people than Abimelech, and he throws down the gauntlet to challenge Abimelech.

Why was Abimelech having such a rough time as leader? He was simply reaping what he sowed. If you recall, we read in Judges 9:5 that Abimelech had murdered 68 of his half-brothers in cold blood, all so he would be assured to come into power rather than one of them. He was now paying the price for his violent actions by the people turning against him.

What have you done in your life that you're facing negative consequences for? Bad decisions lead to bad outcomes; that's how God's natural law works. How are you going to handle those negative consequences?

The Plot Against Abimelech

Judges 9:30-41

When Zebul the governor of the city heard what Gaal son of Ebed said, he was very angry. Under cover he sent messengers to Abimelech, saying, "Gaal son of Ebed and his clan have come to Shechem and are stirring up the city against you. Now then, during the night you and your men should come and lie in wait in the fields. In the morning at sunrise, advance against the city. When Gaal and his men come out against you, seize the opportunity to attack them." So Abimelech and all his troops set out by night and took up concealed positions near Shechem in four companies. Now Gaal son of Ebed had gone out and was standing at the entrance of the city gate just as Abimelech and his troops came out from their hiding place.

When Gaal saw them, he said to Zebul, "Look, people are coming down from the tops of the mountains!"

Zebul replied, "You mistake the shadows of the mountains for men."

But Gaal spoke up again: "Look, people are coming down from the central hill, and a company is coming from the direction of the diviners' tree."

Then Zebul said to him, "Where is your big talk now, you who said, 'Who is Abimelech that we should be subject to him?' Aren't these the men you ridiculed? Go out and fight them!"

So Gaal led out the citizens of Shechem and fought Abimelech. Abimelech chased him all the way to the entrance of the gate, and many were killed as they fled. Then Abimelech stayed in Arumah, and Zebul drove Gaal and his clan out of Shechem. ~ Judges 9:30-41

Abimelech was facing some negative consequences for his violent acts, and a Canaanite man named Gaal challenged his position as ruler. Abimelech didn't live in Shechem where this story takes place, but he had appointed Zebul to be the local ruler there.

Zebul found out about Gaal's challenge to Abimelech's rule, so he does exactly what he's supposed to and informs Abimelech of the plot to overthrow him. Zebul recommends to Abimelech that he do something about this quickly, before the people have a chance to band together for this cause and make things worse. Abimelech does just that and sets out with his army overnight.

Zebul and Gaal are hanging out by the city gate, and Zebul gets worried that Gaal will see Abimelech's army coming and prepare a defense. Zebul tries to distract Gaal, but that doesn't really work. Once Gaal figures out what's going on, Zebul eggs him on and starts trash talking about how he's going to get clobbered.

War breaks out: Abimelech and his army versus Gaal and the people of Shechem who were rallying for the cause of getting Abimelech out of power. Abimelech and Zebul work on getting Gaal and his family out of Shechem so they can't cause any more trouble there.

What can we learn from this story that helps us in our daily lives today? One lesson is that we need to face whatever our problems are. If you have someone in your life that you have a disagreement with, don't just sit back and complain without doing anything. Don't get into an all-out physical war with them like Abimelech did with Gaal, but do confront them in a loving manner. Do so as promptly as possible before the situation gets worse and you're faced with a larger problem later on.

Another lesson we can learn from this passage is about how to be a good employee. Abimelech was Zebul's boss. Zebul could have heard about Gaal's plot and decided to go along with it, to overthrow Abimelech and maybe become the ruler himself. But instead, he informed Abimelech right away and sided with him rather than against him. It's important to have open lines of communication with your employer (or your employees, depending on your situation) and keep them informed of situations that could cause issues later if left unchecked.

How are you like Zebul and Abimelech in your life? Or how are you like Gaal, stirring up trouble for other people? Take a look at your roles in life and ask God for guidance on where you may need to work on your attitude.

The Ambush

Judges 9:42-49

The next day the people of Shechem went out to the fields, and this was reported to Abimelech. So he took his men, divided them into three companies and set an ambush in the fields. When he saw the people coming out of the city, he rose to attack them. Abimelech and the companies with him rushed forward to a position at the entrance of the city gate. Then two companies attacked those in the fields and struck them down. All that day Abimelech pressed his attack against the city until he had captured it and killed its people. Then he destroyed the city and scattered salt over it.
On hearing this, the citizens in the tower of Shechem went into the stronghold of the temple of El-Berith. When Abimelech heard that they had assembled there, he and all his men went up Mount Zalmon. He took an ax and cut off some branches, which he lifted to his shoulders. He ordered the men with him, "Quick! Do what you have seen me do!" So all the men cut branches and followed Abimelech. They piled them against the stronghold and set it on fire with the people still inside. So all the people in the tower of Shechem, about a thousand men and women, also died.
~ Judges 9:42-49

Abimelech and his army have come to Shechem to stop a plot to overthrow him as leader, which they successfully did, running Gaal the Canaanite out of town. What are they doing still staying in Shechem?

Abimelech decided that he needed to punish the citizens of Shechem for their lack of loyalty to him. If he hadn't immediately intervened, it's likely that Gaal would have rallied the people and even more of them would have been fighting against Abimelech. Abimelech decides that one more good ambush should do the trick.

This was all going on during their harvest season. The city of Shechem had walls around it, and only the city proper was inside the walls. The fields where they grew their crops were outside the walls. To harvest their crops, the people had to leave the protection of the city's walls. After Abimelech ran Gaal out of town, the people would not have expected any further military action, and they had to get back to the work of harvesting.

So, what does Abimelech do? He ambushes the unsuspecting civilians of Shechem! While the men were all out working in the fields, Abimelech's army got between them and the city so they were unable to retreat to safety, and he killed them all.

After the ambush of the workers in the fields, Abimelech wasn't done yet. He and his army went to the tower, which was 68 feet wide and 84 feet high. It was located inside the city, and its purpose was for people to take shelter in and defend the city. However, the tower didn't provide enough protection this time; Abimelech and his army set it on fire, which only furthered the mass slaughter and Abimelech's total capture of the city.

It says in verse 45 that "he destroyed the city and scattered salt over it." Scattering salt over it symbolizes the utter destruction of Shechem and its perpetual infertility. There are other references to this in Deuteronomy 29:23 and Psalm 107:33-34. If salt is scattered on plants, that plant will die, and Shechem died. The city wasn't rebuilt until almost 200 years later (1 Kings 12:25).

What can we take away from this story? Abimelech was a ruthless leader. He may have looked good to begin with (for those who weren't paying attention to how he came into power, by killing 68 of his half-brothers), but as time goes on his true character was revealed.

Whenever you are in a situation where you need to vote on or choose a leader, take note of the true character of the candidates. Look at their past actions to see how they handle certain situations. Will he or she be a person who follows God's will? Or will he or she say that up front, but then show their true character and not lead well? Only time will tell, but make sure you look for clues, investigate, and pray that God would guide your heart and the hearts of the future leaders as well.

Abimelech's Just Consequence
Judges 9:50-57

Next Abimelech went to Thebez and besieged it and captured it.
Inside the city, however, was a strong tower, to which all the men
and women—all the people of the city—had fled. They had locked
themselves in and climbed up on the tower roof. Abimelech went to
the tower and attacked it. But as he approached the entrance to the
tower to set it on fire, a woman dropped an upper millstone on his
head and cracked his skull.
Hurriedly he called to his armor-bearer, "Draw your sword and kill
me, so that they can't say, 'A woman killed him.'" So his servant ran
him through, and he died. When the Israelites saw that Abimelech
was dead, they went home.
Thus God repaid the wickedness that Abimelech had done to his
father by murdering his seventy brothers. God also made the people
of Shechem pay for all their wickedness. The curse of Jotham son of
Jerub-Baal came on them.
~ Judges 9:50-57

Abimelech and his army have just decimated the town of Shechem.
Now, they're headed to the next town of Thebez to capture it as well.
We don't know why Abimelech felt the need to take the town of
Thebez as well, except that he was likely being power hungry.

The town of Thebez was around 10 miles to the northeast of
Shechem, but word travels fast. The inhabitants of Thebez had heard
what happened at Shechem, so they were as prepared as they could

be. They all went up to the roof of their strong tower so they could potentially fight back against Abimelech and his army.

The story takes an unexpected twist when a woman drops an upper millstone on Abimelech's head. An upper millstone was around 10" long, and it would go back and forth over the lower millstone, which was larger, as the grain was crushed in the process of milling. At 10" long, this was not a huge stone, and perhaps the woman had it nearby and figured it could be a good weapon.

With factors such as wind and the height from which it was dropped, it would have been nearly impossible for the women to hit Abimelech square on the head except for pure luck - or perhaps God's intervention. This had to be an act of divine retribution, of God's judgment against Abimelech's evil deeds.

Being killed by a woman was considered incredibly disgraceful, and power-hungry and image-conscious Abimelech definitely didn't want that! Since he wasn't dead yet from the impact of the stone, he had his armor bearer actually finish him off with his sword. But, that ended up being essentially irrelevant. The story of Abimelech being killed by a woman was what lived on, and it was even referenced later in Scripture, in 2 Samuel 11:21.

So now that their leader Abimelech was dead, Israel's army had no purpose to stay there, so as it says in verse 55, they simply went home. They had no hard feelings against the people of Thebez; they were only there to follow their leader's desire for power.

Remember way back in Judges 9:1-21 how Abimelech's half-brother, Jotham, warned Israel how they would be cursed through Abimelech if they let him be their leader? That had finally come true, and it was fulfilled in multiple ways. The city of Shechem was destroyed when Abimelech set it on fire, and that fire was likely fed by thorn bushes in the city. In Jotham's curse, he spoke of thorn bushes to represent Abimelech. It all came full circle now, with God providing this judgment up Abimelech for all the evil he had done.

There are always consequences for our actions, both good and bad, and sometimes it takes a while before we see them. The people of Israel allowed Abimelech to become their leader, even though they had already seen the evil he was capable of when he killed 68 of his half-brothers so that he could be the one in charge. Because of this, the town of Shechem and all its inhabitants were completely destroyed. The town of Thebez fared a bit better, and only the buildings of the town and not its people were destroyed. They allowed a man who had already shown his evil character to become their leader, and they paid for it with the consequences later. Abimelech himself reaped the consequences of what he sowed. By killing many, many people, he was killed himself, and in a very disgraceful way.

What are you doing in your life that could lead to negative consequences later on? Take a look at your actions and attitudes today and make whatever changes you need to so that you'll have positive consequences later on.

Worshiping Other Gods
Judges 10:6-9

Again the Israelites did evil in the eyes of the Lord. They served the Baals and the Ashtoreths, and the gods of Aram, the gods of Sidon, the gods of Moab, the gods of the Ammonites and the gods of the Philistines. And because the Israelites forsook the Lord and no longer served him, he became angry with them. He sold them into the hands of the Philistines and the Ammonites, who that year shattered and crushed them. For eighteen years they oppressed all the Israelites on the east side of the Jordan in Gilead, the land of the Amorites. The Ammonites also crossed the Jordan to fight against Judah, Benjamin and Ephraim; Israel was in great distress.
~ Judges 10:6-9

After spending many chapters looking at the stories of Gideon and his son Abimelech in the book of Judges, we're moving on toward the story of Jephthah. In Judges 10:1-5, we see a couple minor judges named Tola and Jair, but they were not significant enough to have much of their legacy recorded in Scripture.

In this passage, we're back to the repeating pattern of the people of Israel in the era of the judges: sin, slavery, supplication, salvation, and silence. In this passage, Israel had against strayed from worshiping the one true God, and they were instead worshiping a whole bunch of other gods. In verse 6 we read, "Again the Israelites did evil in the eyes of the Lord. They served the Baals and the Ashtoreths, and the gods of Aram, the gods of Sidon, the gods of

Moab, the gods of the Ammonites and the gods of the Philistines. And because the Israelites forsook the Lord and no longer served him."

This list of other gods that the Israelites worshiped is the most extensive list throughout Judges. The Baals and the Ashtoreths were worshipped by most of the nations mentioned in this passage who surrounded Israel's territory. The Moabites' god was named Chemosh (Numbers 21:29), the Ammonites' god was named Molek (1 Kings 11:5), and the Philistines' god was named Dagon (Judges 16:23).

When Israel doesn't serve the one true God, God gets angry with them for blatantly disobeying His commandments. Exodus 20:3 seems pretty clear: "You shall have no other gods before me." That seems like a pretty easy one to remember, but we always forget that today, too. While I don't worship a god by name like Dagon or Molek, I have times in my life where I put other people and things before God, thus making them little gods in my life. I would guess you've done that too, if you take an honest look at your life.

So, when Israel turns away from God (again), He allows them to be enslaved and oppressed by their enemies (verses 7-8). This particular incident happened around the year 1096 BC. Previously, during Gideon's time, the Israelites were badly oppressed by the Midianites. Now, however, the oppression was even worse. Now it was both the Ammonites and Philistines oppressing them, and they were just as evil as the Midianites, if not more so.

The recurring theme in the book of Judges is that while God is good, as humans we will reap what we sow. Israel was often sowing disobedience to God by worshiping other gods, and therefore they were reaping the consequences of their actions. While God will continue to forgive them when they are finally sorry for their actions, that doesn't mean He'll lessen the punishment. In fact, He seems to be increasing the harshness of the punishments as they continue to not learn their lesson.

What are you doing in your life where you may be repeating the same sin over and over again? What do you need to repent from, and finally learn the lesson that God is trying to teach you - before the consequences get even worse?

God Gets Snarky
Judges 10:10-18

Then the Israelites cried out to the Lord, "We have sinned against you, forsaking our God and serving the Baals."
The Lord replied, "When the Egyptians, the Amorites, the Ammonites, the Philistines, the Sidonians, the Amalekites and the Maonites oppressed you and you cried to me for help, did I not save you from their hands? But you have forsaken me and served other gods, so I will no longer save you. Go and cry out to the gods you have chosen. Let them save you when you are in trouble!"
But the Israelites said to the Lord, "We have sinned. Do with us whatever you think best, but please rescue us now." Then they got rid of the foreign gods among them and served the Lord. And he could bear Israel's misery no longer.
When the Ammonites were called to arms and camped in Gilead, the Israelites assembled and camped at Mizpah. The leaders of the people of Gilead said to each other, "Whoever will take the lead in attacking the Ammonites will be head over all who live in Gilead."
~ Judges 10:10-18

In the last chapter, we saw how the people of Israel were again disobeying God and worshiping false gods. Because of that, God allowed them to be oppressed by the Ammonites and the Philistines. The Israelites are still stuck in their recurring pattern of sin, slavery, supplication, salvation, and silence.

Now in this passage, we finally see the people crying out to God for deliverance (the supplication part of the pattern). We see them crying out in both verse 10 and again in verse 15. Israel had repeated this pattern so often that they definitely did not deserve God's salvation. He had saved them so many times, and they kept turning back to their old ways of serving false gods.

At this point, we know that God had delivered them from at least 7 oppressors. Through Moses, God released them from oppression and slavery to the Egyptians. They were delivered from the Amorite kings Sihon and Og in Joshua 2:10. The judge Ehud killed Eglon, the king of the Ammonites / Moab, in Judges 3:12-30. The judge Shamgar defeated the Philistines previously in Judges 3:31. Deborah and Barak delivered Israel from the Canaanites and Sisera in Judges 4. The Amalekites helped out the Moabites in Judges 3:13. Finally, through Gideon, God delivered them from the Midianites, also known as the Maonites (Judges 6).

You know how when someone keeps doing the same annoying or hurtful thing to you, you tend to get frustrated and angry with them? God got to that point with the Israelites, too. This pattern had gone on so many times. God gets a little snarky with them in verses 13-14: "But you have forsaken me and served other gods, so I will no longer save you. Go and cry out to the gods you have chosen. Let them save you when you are in trouble!" If they obviously think these other gods are so great that they're worshiping them instead of God, why not cry out to them for salvation, right?

But Israel continues to plead with God. They tried to show God that they really meant it this time by throwing out their idols (verse 16). And, being the loving God that He is, God finally relented and begins working to save them yet again.

The stage is now set for a battle against the Ammonites, but Israel didn't have a commander for their army. They improvise and see who would prove themselves to be fit for the job. We'll see how that plays out in the next chapter.

The Israelites were taking advantage of God's grace by continually doing what they knew was wrong and expecting God's forgiveness. This attitude is not just in the book of Judges, however. Paul spoke against this in his letter to the Romans: "What shall we say, then? Shall we go on sinning so that grace may increase? By no means! We are those who have died to sin; how can we live in it any longer?" (Romans 6:1-2). We should not knowingly sin, just because we also know that God will give us grace and forgive us.

What sins are you committing in your life that you know are wrong, but you do them anyway? While God will forgive you of them when you are truly sorry and repent of them, don't be like Israel and continue to commit them anyway. Ask the Holy Spirit for help to turn away from those sins for good.

Meet Jephthah

Judges 11:1-11

*Jephthah the Gileadite was a mighty warrior. His father was Gilead;
his mother was a prostitute. Gilead's wife also bore him sons, and
when they were grown up, they drove Jephthah away. "You are not
going to get any inheritance in our family," they said, "because you
are the son of another woman." So Jephthah fled from his brothers
and settled in the land of Tob, where a gang of scoundrels gathered
around him and followed him.*

*Some time later, when the Ammonites were fighting against Israel,
the elders of Gilead went to get Jephthah from the land of Tob.
"Come," they said, "be our commander, so we can fight the
Ammonites."*

*Jephthah said to them, "Didn't you hate me and drive me from my
father's house? Why do you come to me now, when you're in
trouble?"*

*The elders of Gilead said to him, "Nevertheless, we are turning to
you now; come with us to fight the Ammonites, and you will be head
over all of us who live in Gilead."*

*Jephthah answered, "Suppose you take me back to fight the
Ammonites and the Lord gives them to me—will I really be your
head?"*

*The elders of Gilead replied, "The Lord is our witness; we will
certainly do as you say." So Jephthah went with the elders of Gilead,
and the people made him head and commander over them. And he
repeated all his words before the Lord in Mizpah.*

~ Judges 11:1-11

Israel is being oppressed by the Ammonites and Philistines, and in the previous passage, we saw that they were finally crying out to God for help, and God decided to deliver them. But, they needed a commander for their army, so now we come to the story of Jephthah.

First, we need to know Jephthah's background. He was from an upper-class family of that time, and he was named after a famous ancestor - the grandson of Manasseh, who was the son Joseph (of the "coat of many colors" fame). But, Jephthah was an illegitimate son, being born from a prostitute, so he ranked at the very bottom of the family hierarchy. Because of this, he ended up having to run away from his family.

While away from his family, Jephthah established his reputation as a skilled fighter. Now that Israel needed a skilled fighter like Jephthah, his brothers saw his value and wanted his help, after running him off years earlier. Naturally, Jephthah is bitter about this history between him and his brothers (verse 7). They expect him to help them, after they were so mean to him? Really??

To try and convince Jephthah to help them out, the elders of Israel promised him a position as ruler of Gilead after the battle (verse 8). In verse 9, Jephthah shows his deep faith in God: if Israel wins the battle, it's not because of his skill but because of the Lord's doing. So, Jephthah was made the commander of the army.

Jephthah was considered the least of his family, but God clearly has a plan for his life. You may think that God could never use you because of your situation or what you've been through in life, but as we'll see as we continue in this story, God will use Jephthah and God can use you, too. God will do mighty things through your life if you're obedient to Him, even if you have a troubled past or a lowly upbringing. None of that matters to God; you are His child and He would love to invite you into what He is doing in your life and use you for His mighty purposes. Will you let Him?

Make Discussion, Not War
Judges 11:12-17

*Then Jephthah sent messengers to the Ammonite king with the
question: "What do you have against me that you have attacked my
country?"*
*The king of the Ammonites answered Jephthah's messengers, "When
Israel came up out of Egypt, they took away my land from the Arnon
to the Jabbok, all the way to the Jordan. Now give it back
peaceably."*
Jephthah sent back messengers to the Ammonite king, saying:
*"This is what Jephthah says: Israel did not take the land of Moab or
the land of the Ammonites. But when they came up out of Egypt,
Israel went through the wilderness to the Red Sea and on to Kadesh.
Then Israel sent messengers to the king of Edom, saying, 'Give us
permission to go through your country,' but the king of Edom would
not listen. They sent also to the king of Moab, and he refused. So
Israel stayed at Kadesh."*
~ Judges 11:12-17

At this point in the story, Jephthah had been made ruler of Israel's
army. The Ammonites were threatening Israel, so they needed a
good commander to make them successful in the impending war.
Jephthah is taking charge and first trying to get to the bottom of what
the problem is with the Ammonites.

In the start of this passage, Jephthah asks the Ammonite king why
they're attacking Israel. Instead of just jumping right into battle,

Jephthah goes for diplomacy and tries to reason out the conflict first. Perhaps it was just a simple miscommunication and they don't need to start a war.

The king's reply indicates that the Ammonites don't want war either. They believed that Israel took their land away, so they simply want it back. There's no need for a war, just give their land back and everybody is happy, right?

Well, it's not quite that easy. Jephthah begins to give a history of how Israel came to occupy this land in the first place. They captured it honestly and did not violate anyone's rights. This discussion will continue in the next section, and Jephthah will give even more reasons that Israel should keep this land.

So how does this apply to us today? Odds are you're not in any territorial dispute like that, and if so, we have much better record keeping and processes today to solve such matters. But look at how Jephthah addresses this potential conflict. Remember, he was a very skilled warrior. He could have just said, "Ok Israel, let's all gear up for battle and wipe the Ammonites off the face of the earth!" But he didn't. Instead, he tries to spare both parties the agony and loss that would occur with war by being reasonable and discussing the matter first, to see if they can come to some kind agreement without the bloodshed.

While most disagreements in our lives don't get to the point of bloodshed (hopefully!), this is a good principle to remember. Before you let your anger and emotions get the best of you, try to discuss the matter calmly. Listen to the other person's perspective and try to understand where they're coming from, and calmly share your side of the story too. Don't just jump into an argument in anger, but first try to work with the other party. It's always better to try and work things out through good, honest communication rather than hostile fighting.

Jephthah's Negotiations
Judges 11:18-28

*"Next they traveled through the wilderness, skirted the lands of
Edom and Moab, passed along the eastern side of the country of
Moab, and camped on the other side of the Arnon. They did not enter
the territory of Moab, for the Arnon was its border.
Then Israel sent messengers to Sihon king of the Amorites, who ruled
in Heshbon, and said to him, Let us pass through your country to our
own place.' Sihon, however, did not trust Israel to pass through his
territory. He mustered all his troops and encamped at Jahaz and
fought with Israel.
"Then the Lord, the God of Israel, gave Sihon and his whole army
into Israel's hands, and they defeated them. Israel took over all the
land of the Amorites who lived in that country, capturing all of it
from the Arnon to the Jabbok and from the desert to the Jordan.
Now since the Lord, the God of Israel, has driven the Amorites out
before his people Israel, what right have you to take it over? Will
you not take what your god Chemosh gives you? Likewise, whatever
the Lord our God has given us, we will possess. Are you any better
than Balak son of Zippor, king of Moab? Did he ever quarrel with
Israel or fight with them? For three hundred years Israel occupied
Heshbon, Aroer, the surrounding settlements and all the towns along
the Arnon. Why didn't you retake them during that time? I have not
wronged you, but you are doing me wrong by waging war against
me. Let the Lord, the Judge, decide the dispute this day between the
Israelites and the Ammonites."*

*The king of Ammon, however, paid no attention to the message
Jephthah sent him.*
~ Judges 11:18-28

At this point in the narrative, Jephthah is continuing to explain to the
Ammonites why Israel is occupying this particular area of land, after
the Ammonites threatened to take it away from them.

When Israel had first come to this land, it was occupied by the
Amorites. Israel fought against them, and Israel clearly won control
of this land. There should be no conflict with the Ammonites or the
Moabites now, since Israel had clearly won possession of this land.

Back in those days, when there was a war, it was considered to be
between the gods of the two lands. It was clear that God had given
Israel this land by winning the battle for them. Therefore, the
Ammonites should have no right to take it away. In verse 24,
Jephthah refers to the god Chemosh. Chemosh was actually the god
of Moab, but the nations of Moab and Ammon were very closely
linked.

Finally, Jephthah gives one more argument for Israel's right to
occupy the land: length of time. Israel had been in that land for over
300 years! That's a pretty long time, and that should show that they
have a valid claim to it.

Jephthah closes his discussion by saying that God is the one who
will decide who gets this land in verse 27: "I have not wronged you,
but you are doing me wrong by waging war against me. Let the
Lord, the Judge, decide the dispute this day between the Israelites
and the Ammonites." Jephthah shows his faith in God here, that
whatever God decides, that's the way things should be.

So, Jephthah spends all this time clearly stating his argument to the
king of Ammon, and he sets up a pretty good case for why Israel
should stay in the land and Ammon should just drop the issue. But
then in verse 28, "The king of Ammon, however, paid no attention to
the message Jephthah sent him."

Jephthah truly tried to work things out before going to battle with Ammon. But even when we try our best to have a civil discussion to avoid a worse argument, there are times that the other party just won't listen. When these times happen, that's when we need to do as Jephthah did, and let God be the judge. Listen to what God is telling you to do in that situation and trust Him that He is in control and will judge the situation and work out the outcome fairly - at least fairly according to God's plan.

Jephthah Makes His Vow

Judges 11:29-33

Then the Spirit of the Lord came on Jephthah. He crossed Gilead and Manasseh, passed through Mizpah of Gilead, and from there he advanced against the Ammonites. And Jephthah made a vow to the Lord: "If you give the Ammonites into my hands, whatever comes out of the door of my house to meet me when I return in triumph from the Ammonites will be the Lord's, and I will sacrifice it as a burnt offering."
Then Jephthah went over to fight the Ammonites, and the Lord gave them into his hands. He devastated twenty towns from Aroer to the vicinity of Minnith, as far as Abel Keramim. Thus Israel subdued Ammon.
~ Judges 11:29-33

Jephthah has been trying to reason with the king of Ammon in order to avoid war, but the king has essentially ignored him. Fortunately, Jephthah has God's Spirit with him as they go into battle. Jephthah did what he could to try and avoid a bloody battle, but now it has become unavoidable. So, Jephthah begins gathering troops from his fellow Israelite tribes of Gad and Manasseh.

Jephthah really wants victory, even though he knows God's Spirit is with them, so he makes a vow to the Lord. It says in verses 30-31, "And Jephthah made a vow to the Lord: 'If you give the Ammonites into my hands, whatever comes out of the door of my house to meet me when I return in triumph from the Ammonites will be the Lord's, and I will sacrifice it as a burnt offering.'" The intention of this vow was to show Jephthah's honor to God, but instead it could be indicating his lack of belief. Did Jephthah have a lack of faith? Or was this his way of saying that he totally trusted God?

In the vow, this NIV translation says, "whatever comes out the door..." That could also be translated as "whoever," as the language isn't clear on that. Was this intended to be a human sacrifice, or an animal one? The text isn't clear on that. An animal sacrifice would not be an unusual thing, since those happened all the time. A human sacrifice, however, would be very unique. Even back then, that was considered to be murder. Sacrificing humans was clearly forbidden in the Law of Moses (see Exodus 20:13, Leviticus 18:21, and Deuteronomy 12:31). Killing another person, for whatever reason, would not have been ok with God. Many pagan nations surrounding Israel at the time would sacrifice their children for religious purposes in worshiping their pagan gods, so that may have been an influence on this. We really don't have enough detail to say for sure. What's clear is that victory in this battle was SO important to Jephthah that he was willing to kill for it.

As it turns out, Israel was given victory in this battle. Many Ammonites died in the battle, but the land officially belonged to Israel again and they had gotten rid of the threat. What happened with Jephthah's vow? We'll find out in the next chapter.

While this is an interesting story from Israel's history, what does it have to do with us today? One thing that is clear is that we should not make vows like this one. We have passages in the New Testament that discourage this sort of thing. Matthew 5:34 says, "But I tell you, do not swear an oath at all: either by heaven, for it is God's throne." James 5:12 says, "Above all, my brothers and sisters, do not swear—not by heaven or by earth or by anything else. All you need to say is a simple 'Yes' or 'No.' Otherwise you will be condemned." We should simply keep our word, then people will be able to count on us; oaths or vows are not typically necessary.

Jephthah making this vow is like he's trying to make a deal with God. He says something rash without necessarily thinking it all the way through. Have you ever done that in your life? Maybe you've committed to something that sounded great, but then once it comes down to it, you really don't want to follow through. Or maybe you've pleaded with God: "God, if you get me out of this situation (usually one that I've gotten myself into), I'll read my Bible every day and go to church every Sunday!" While these may be heartfelt in the moment, often they're just rash statements that we either break later or regret making in the first place.

Be careful about what you commit to; make sure that you can keep your word in all situations, and part of that is by not being hasty in our statements.

Jephthah Keeps His Vow

Judges 11:34-40

When Jephthah returned to his home in Mizpah, who should come out to meet him but his daughter, dancing to the sound of timbrels! She was an only child. Except for her he had neither son nor daughter. When he saw her, he tore his clothes and cried, "Oh no, my daughter! You have brought me down and I am devastated. I have made a vow to the Lord that I cannot break."

"My father," she replied, "you have given your word to the Lord. Do to me just as you promised, now that the Lord has avenged you of your enemies, the Ammonites. But grant me this one request," she said. "Give me two months to roam the hills and weep with my friends, because I will never marry."

"You may go," he said. And he let her go for two months. She and her friends went into the hills and wept because she would never marry. After the two months, she returned to her father, and he did to her as he had vowed. And she was a virgin.

From this comes the Israelite tradition that each year the young women of Israel go out for four days to commemorate the daughter of Jephthah the Gileadite.

~ Judges 11:34-40

Previously, we read about the vow Jephthah made regarding the battle with the Ammonites. "And Jephthah made a vow to the Lord: 'If you give the Ammonites into my hands, whatever comes out of the door of my house to meet me when I return in triumph from the Ammonites will be the Lord's, and I will sacrifice it as a burnt offering'" (Judges 11:30-31). Since God granted Israel victory in the battle, Jephthah had vowed to kill whatever (or whoever) came out to meet him when he returned home.

Jephthah was blinded by the desire for victory, and we can pretty safely assume that he never thought it would be a close family member who he would have to sacrifice. But, his own daughter, his only child, was the one to walk through that door first. She had completely unknowingly brought disaster to her father and their family.

Because of this vow that Jephthah had made, likely foolishly, both the Ammonites and Jephthah's family experienced bitter distress. Many Ammonites lost their lives in the battle, and now Jephthah had unintentionally vowed to kill his own daughter! This was a tricky dilemma, because it's a sin to break a vow to God (Numbers 30:2), but in this situation it was actually a greater sin to fulfill it by killing a person (Exodus 20:13).

Amazingly, Jephthah's daughter seems ok with what has to happen. Her father has to keep the vow that he made. We see a similar situation much earlier in Scripture, where Abraham needs to follow God's command by sacrificing his only son, Isaac (Genesis 22). Isaac was a willing victim, though fortunately, God stopped Abraham before he actually killed his son.

Later in the New Testament, we see that Jesus is a willing victim for all of us. Because mankind sinned, the penalty of death needed to be paid for all of us. The only person who could pay that penalty fully was Jesus Christ. He willingly allowed Himself to be the ultimate victim, to be killed in a very violent death, so that we could be saved.

Jephthah needing to sacrifice his daughter, however, was not to save anyone from their sins. It was the result of a foolish statement that he had made in the heat of the moment. Jephthah's desire for victory in one battle caused his only daughter to lose her life! Jephthah did end up killing his daughter, as best as we can tell from the Bible. He felt that he had to do it because of his vow.

It would have been better to simply trust God for the outcome of the battle and not make this vow in the first place. An innocent life would have been spared if Jephthah had committed to fully relying on God rather than trying to bargain with God and influence it himself.

Have you done this in your life? Have you made a rash decision or said things in the heat of emotion that you now regret? Our actions always have consequences (that's God's natural law), and our foolish actions almost always come with negative consequences. If we put our trust fully in God, then we will be following His course for our life. We wouldn't have to worry about making stupid decisions if we're walking in step with God and living the life that He calls us to live. Be careful about what you do and say, but always trust in God fully.

Shibboleth

Judges 12:1-7

The Ephraimite forces were called out, and they crossed over to Zaphon. They said to Jephthah, "Why did you go to fight the Ammonites without calling us to go with you? We're going to burn down your house over your head."

Jephthah answered, "I and my people were engaged in a great struggle with the Ammonites, and although I called, you didn't save me out of their hands. When I saw that you wouldn't help, I took my life in my hands and crossed over to fight the Ammonites, and the Lord gave me the victory over them. Now why have you come up today to fight me?"

Jephthah then called together the men of Gilead and fought against Ephraim. The Gileadites struck them down because the Ephraimites had said, "You Gileadites are renegades from Ephraim and Manasseh." The Gileadites captured the fords of the Jordan leading to Ephraim, and whenever a survivor of Ephraim said, "Let me cross over," the men of Gilead asked him, "Are you an Ephraimite?" If he replied, "No," they said, "All right, say 'Shibboleth.'" If he said, "Sibboleth," because he could not pronounce the word correctly, they seized him and killed him at the fords of the Jordan. Forty-two thousand Ephraimites were killed at that time.

Jephthah led Israel six years. Then Jephthah the Gileadite died and was buried in a town in Gilead.

~ Judges 12:1-7

Jephthah has gone to war with the Ammonites, God gave them victory, Jephthah had to kill his daughter, and the bad stuff just keeps on coming for Jephthah. Now, the tribe of Ephraim is mad at him.

Ephraim had been mad at Gideon previously for not being invited to participate in the battle against Midian. But then Gideon had gotten them involved, so all was well (Judges 8:1-3). Now, however, this dispute with Ephraim ended up in a civil war between the tribes of Ephraim and Manasseh. They're both tribes of the same nation (Israel), and interestingly both of those tribes were descended from the sons of Joseph.

The fact of the matter is that God granted Jephthah victory over the Ammonites. Ephraim had no reason to be jealous for that; they worshiped the same God and were part of Israel as well. But the tribe of Ephraim was jealous anyway.

These two tribes of Ephraim and Manasseh were close geographically, but they were separated by the Jordan River (one on the east and one on the west). Because of this separation, each tribe had a slightly different dialect. In the Hebrew language, there are two letters called sin and shin (say them like "seen" and "sheen"). The letters look identical, similar to a W, except for the placement of a dot. If the dot is on the left side of the W, then it's a sin (pronounced like an "s"); if the dot is on the right, then it's a shin (pronounced like an "sh"). It's not a huge difference, but the using a sin instead of a shin can change the word entirely, as they are considered two distinct letters.

So, to tell which side any given person was on (Ephraim vs Manasseh), they would be asked to pronounce the word 'Sibboleth.' Depending on whether a person pronounced it with a 'S' sound or a 'Sh' sound, they'd know if you were "us" or "them." This could possibly be compared to the U.S. with northerners and southerners. Ask someone what they call a group of people, and if they say "y'all" then they're more likely from the south.

But back to the point. Two tribes, under the same nation and worshiping the same God, were having a civil war. Because of this division, 42,000 people in Ephraim lost their lives! Jephthah was clearly vindicated as the leader, but his actions cost the loss of much life - the Ammonites during the battle, Jephthah's own daughter, and now thousands of Ephraimites as well. That's a pretty big deal, and a lot of negative consequences for some actions.

While the pronunciation difference may seem silly to us today (I'm from Michigan and I occasionally do say "y'all"), we have just as much division today as Israel had then, if not more. Instead of asking each other how to pronounce a word, what about these topics: who you vote for in a presidential election, what's your position on homosexual marriage, do you believe in creation or evolution, etc. We have SO many dividing issues, yet we're all called to be one nation, united under God. Fortunately, in recent history our divisions haven't killed 42,000 people like with the tribe of Ephraim, but we humans have a way of letting things get out of hand.

Can't we all just get along? We're all humans, created to love and serve the God of the universe. We're all sinful, unfortunately, which causes divisions among us, but that choice is ours to make. Make the choice to be unified under God with your fellow humans.

What Is a Nazirite?

What is a Nazirite? Isn't that something from the Old Testament? Why is that something we should care about today? Read on and find out.

Yes, a Nazirite is something that comes out of the Old Testament. It's part of the law that God gave to the people of Israel as recorded in the book of Numbers, specifically Numbers 6:1-21. To summarize that passage for you, being a Nazirite was a vow that a person would take. This vow would involve 3 things:
1. No wine or strong drink
2. No cutting your hair
3. No contact with anything dead

The vow of being a Nazirite could last any amount of time, either a set period or for a person's entire life. We see 3 people in Scripture who had the Nazirite vow for life: Samson (Judges 13:4-5), Samuel (1 Samuel 1:11), and John the Baptist (Luke 1:15). If you look at the context of each of those passages, the instructions for the Nazirite vow were given to the mothers before their sons were even born. We also see the apostle Paul taking a Nazirite vow for a time during his ministry in Corinth (Acts 18:18), and another time later on (Acts 21:23-26). Generally, the vow would last anywhere from 30-100 days.

When a Nazirite vow would be ended (for anyone taking it on a temporary basis), the former Nazirite would have to go to the temple to make some sacrifices: a male lamb less than a year old, a female lamb less than a year old, and a ram. These animals would be sacrificed by the priest, and the Nazirite would now be allowed to cut his hair and throw it into the fire.

But why is this important for us today? One primary purpose of the Nazirite vow is to show worship of and complete allegiance to God. This is similar to how today people will refrain from certain activities (drinking, wild partying, dancing in some Christian denominations, etc.). They don't necessarily refrain from those things because they don't like them; instead they refrain to honor God and as a way to worship Him with their lives. The Nazirite vow is just one way to deny the desires of our human nature to follow God more fully. This vow would also cause the Nazirite to stand out physically from the other people as well, especially for men, since they wouldn't cut their hair.

I'm not saying that we all need to become Nazirites today, but what are you doing to honor God with your life? Do you deny yourself from things you desire, so that you can follow God better? Are there certain things about your appearance or the way you live your life that show people your life is fully devoted to God? Think about what you might do to honor God with your life more fully.

Samson's Birth

Judges 13:1-25

Grab your Bible and read the passage of Judges 13:1-25 now. This is the passage that leads up to and includes the birth of Samson.

As is fairly typical for the book of Judges, in verse 1 we see that again Israel turned away from God and did evil. They were delivered into the hands of the Philistines, and they needed another judge to help them turn back to God. Most of the judges we've read about were already adults before they got called into service by God, but here we see how God called Samson to be a judge even before he was born! Samson is set apart and special from even before his conception.

Being barren and having no children was a disgrace for women in that time, so this was a huge blessing and a great ray of hope in the lives of Manoah and his wife. Finding out they were going to be parents at all was a huge deal, and especially that their son would be no ordinary person. To have this news revealed to them by an angel was also very special. This happened to Hagar (the servant who had a son, Ishmael, with Abraham) back in Genesis 16:11, and an angel would also announce to Mary that she would become pregnant with Jesus.

The other special aspect of this soon-to-be-born child was that the angel commanded his parents that he be a Nazirite. As we saw in the last chapter, the vow of a Nazirite requires 3 things: no wine or strong drink, no cutting your hair, and no contact with anything dead. Manoah's wife was also supposed to abide by the Nazirite rules while she was pregnant, since that way the baby growing inside her would be abiding by that vow too.

This angelic visitor only announced the upcoming child to the mother, so when she tells Manoah about it, he's concerned it's not authentic. For the sake of authenticity, they need to have a name of this man / angel / visitor, so the fact that a name was not given discounts it somewhat. But believing that this could be true, Manoah also gets a little freaked out about the responsibility of raising and parenting such a special child. He prays for a second visit from the angel, which does happen. This shows a lack of faith on Manoah's part that he needed to confirm it with his own eyes, but that's not unusual for us humans. Even Gideon needed more convincing back in Judges 6:36-40.

During this second visit, Manoah tries to find out the angel's name in verses 17-18. The angel replies that his name is "beyond understanding," so that really didn't help Manoah. But when they went to sacrifice the burnt offering, that's when they got their proof - the angel goes up with the smoke! Manoah and his wife realized who had been in their presence, and Manoah thought he would surely die for seeing God, until his wife calmed his fears.

After all of that ordeal, we see at the end of the passage that Samson is born and grows up. His name literally means "sun."

The previous judge over Israel was Jephthah, and we can see a lot of contrast between their two stories. Remember how Jephthah was born of a prostitute and disgraced by his own family? Samson's birth was foretold by an angel and he had godly parents who loved him. He was unique in being dedicated to God as a Nazirite for his whole life, and he even experienced the power of God's Spirit as a young man. But upbringing isn't everything; Jephthah turned out to be a mighty warrior for Israel, and Samson's life becomes marked by disobedience and tragedy as we'll see as we continue through his story.

So, what's the moral of this story for us? The people of Israel had turned away from God (again) and needed someone to help them come back to God. God provided Samson for them as a judge, though he had to be born and grow up before he could truly accomplish this purpose in his life.

Being childless was a big problem for Manoah and his wife, and God provided a son for them. God will provide for our needs, but it will always be according to His timing and His plan. Did Israel want to be under the oppression of the Philistines for many years? Not really, even though it wasn't as bad as the Midianites had been in Gideon's day. But it was God's timing to have Samson born when he was and in the manner that he was in order to fulfill God's good purposes.

What's going on in your life that you'd like God to take care of for you? Remember that God will always work in His timing, and that doesn't necessarily match up with ours. But if something is meant to happen in God's plan, you can count on the fact that it will happen exactly when and how God wants it to.

Samson Chooses His Bride
Judges 14:1-4

Samson went down to Timnah and saw there a young Philistine
woman. When he returned, he said to his father and mother, "I have
seen a Philistine woman in Timnah; now get her for me as my wife."
His father and mother replied, "Isn't there an acceptable woman
among your relatives or among all our people? Must you go to the
uncircumcised Philistines to get a wife?"
But Samson said to his father, "Get her for me. She's the right one
for me." (His parents did not know that this was from the Lord, who
was seeking an occasion to confront the Philistines; for at that time
they were ruling over Israel.)
~ Judges 14:1-4

Samson's childhood was evidently uneventful, as we now pick up
his story when he's a young man getting ready to marry.

During this time, Israel was occupied by the Philistines. The city of
Timnah was about 4 miles away from where Samson lived, and it
was still very much Israelite territory even though there were many
Philistines living there. The Philistine occupation of Israel was much
more peaceful than previous oppressions, and the people were able
to intermingle freely.

In that culture, marriages were almost always arranged by the
parents. Samson choosing his own bride was a very unusual thing,
but then he was an unusual person, having been set apart as a

Nazirite even before his birth. Samson allowed his parents to make the actual arrangements for the wedding, but he wanted to choose his bride for himself.

At first, Samson's parents objected because of God's commands to not intermarry with non-Israelites, as in Deuteronomy 7:1-3, even though that passage does not specifically list Philistines. The Philistines were foreigners who did not worship the one true God whom Israel worshipped. When his parents suggest marrying a "relative," they don't mean his first cousin or something like that; they simply mean a woman from their tribe of Israelites.

Samson was determined to have the woman from Timnah as his bride, so eventually his parents reluctantly gave in. They were certain Samson would be ruining his life with that choice. But what they didn't know was that God was already at work through this situation to redeem Israel from the Philistines.

While Samson wouldn't normally have the opportunity to choose his own bride in that culture, here his parents reluctantly allowed him that opportunity, even if they thought it meant his life would be ruined. We are all given free will by our good God so that we can make whatever choice we choose in all areas of life. We can choose to follow Him or we can choose to disobey Him; it's our choice, but we need to be prepared to face the consequences of whatever choice we make according to God's natural law.

Fortunately, just like Samson's decision to marry the woman from Timnah, God can and will use any choice we make for His purposes. Even if it looks like we're making a mess of our lives, God is so good that He can redeem those bad choices for His purposes, especially if we turn to obeying Him later on once we realize how much we've messed up.

Want a real-life example of this? I would encourage you to check out a book called No Reason to Live, written by my friend Scott Mason (you can find it on Amazon.com). Scott made a lot of bad choices in his life, but when he finally turned his life over to God, God has used him in many ways to spread the Gospel message and help people making similar bad choices.

How are the choices you make affecting your life? Are you allowing God to use your choices for His purposes in your life?

Samson and the Lion
Judges 14:5-9

Samson went down to Timnah together with his father and mother. As they approached the vineyards of Timnah, suddenly a young lion came roaring toward him. The Spirit of the Lord came powerfully upon him so that he tore the lion apart with his bare hands as he might have torn a young goat. But he told neither his father nor his mother what he had done. Then he went down and talked with the woman, and he liked her.

Some time later, when he went back to marry her, he turned aside to look at the lion's carcass, and in it he saw a swarm of bees and some honey. He scooped out the honey with his hands and ate as he went along. When he rejoined his parents, he gave them some, and they too ate it. But he did not tell them that he had taken the honey from the lion's carcass.

~ Judges 14:5-9

Samson was determined to marry a Philistine woman from the city of Timnah in Israel. On this particular day, he and his parents were on their way to Timnah to discuss the marriage plans.

On the way there, a young lion comes toward Samson and he rips it apart with his bare hands! While this sounds pretty impressive, it's actually not a good thing because of the Nazirite vow that was put on his life before he was born. Remember that the Nazirite vow requires that he not have contact with anything dead, and if he killed a lion then he must have had to touch it while it was dead. He also violated

Jewish cleanliness laws by coming into contact with the lion's bodily fluids.

Note that we see in the text how Samson's parents didn't see this encounter with the lion, and he didn't tell them what he had done. More on that in a bit.

While in Timnah, Samson reaffirmed his desire to marry the Philistine woman. But on the way back home, he comes into contact with the dead lion again! He obviously had to touch the dead body in order to eat the honey from the swarm of bees in the lion's carcass. This was still not allowed under his Nazirite vow, and his parents still didn't know that he broke that vow in this way.

At this point we don't see any immediate negative consequences for Samson's disobedience and the breaking of his Nazirite vows, but he still should have known better. Samson thought he could get away with the sin when no one saw him do it.

What sins do you have in your life that are like that? If nobody sees me steal this item from the store, it's ok, right? What if nobody hears that swear word you utter? Or what if no one else knows how you lusted over that cute other person while married to your spouse? The truth is, God knows. God knows every thought you think, every word you say, and every action you do (or don't do). The requirement for something being a sin is not whether it's observed by another person or not; the standard for determining sin is God's law.

Do you think you can get away with sin when no one sees you do it? Pray for God to help you overcome temptation when it comes upon you, whether you're with others or by yourself, so that you can maintain a life pleasing to God.

Samson's Riddle

Judges 14:10-20

Now his father went down to see the woman. And there Samson held a feast, as was customary for young men. When the people saw him, they chose thirty men to be his companions.

"Let me tell you a riddle," Samson said to them. "If you can give me the answer within the seven days of the feast, I will give you thirty linen garments and thirty sets of clothes. If you can't tell me the answer, you must give me thirty linen garments and thirty sets of clothes."

"Tell us your riddle," they said. "Let's hear it."

He replied, "Out of the eater, something to eat; out of the strong, something sweet."

For three days they could not give the answer.

On the fourth day, they said to Samson's wife, "Coax your husband into explaining the riddle for us, or we will burn you and your father's household to death. Did you invite us here to steal our property?"

Then Samson's wife threw herself on him, sobbing, "You hate me! You don't really love me. You've given my people a riddle, but you haven't told me the answer."

"I haven't even explained it to my father or mother," he replied, "so why should I explain it to you?" She cried the whole seven days of the feast. So on the seventh day he finally told her, because she continued to press him. She in turn explained the riddle to her people.

Before sunset on the seventh day the men of the town said to him,

"What is sweeter than honey? What is stronger than a lion?"
Samson said to them, "If you had not plowed with my heifer, you
would not have solved my riddle."
Then the Spirit of the Lord came powerfully upon him. He went
down to Ashkelon, struck down thirty of their men, stripped them of
everything and gave their clothes to those who had explained the
riddle. Burning with anger, he returned to his father's home. And
Samson's wife was given to one of his companions who had attended
him at the feast.
~ Judges 14:10-20

Samson married the Philistine woman from Timnah, and as was the
custom, their wedding feast was going on and lasting 7 days. The 30
companions that Samson had were sort of like groomsmen that we
have in weddings today. The riddle that Samson gives them was
mostly for entertainment purposes, but it was also a competition of
wits between Samson the Israelite and the Philistines. Clothing was
highly valued then, so the 30 sets of clothing that was wagered was a
really big deal.

After 3 days, the Philistine men were getting nervous that they
couldn't figure it out, and they were worried that they may have to
pay the high price. So what do they do? They threaten Samson's
wife to try and get the answer from him. After much nagging,
Samson finally gives in and gives her the answer, which she
immediately passes on to the men. Samson accuses them
(accurately) of not playing fair. In order to pay his debt, he travels 20
miles away to the key Philistine city of Ashkelon where he robs 30
men of their clothing.

At this point, the marriage between Samson and his wife had not yet
been consummated, so it was not yet considered a legal marriage.
His wife's father decided that Samson was not the man for her
daughter, so he gives her to one of the groomsmen in marriage so
she wouldn't be disgraced by Samson's actions.

Samson tried to be witty and get some extra goods from this riddle
challenge, but in the end, it cost him dearly - his wife, his dignity,
and now he has robbed 30 men, too!

All of our actions have consequences. Samson chose to give the riddle challenge with its steep price, and he chose to give in to his wife's nagging, and then he paid for it by coming away unmarried and disgraced.

What choices are you making in life that could have negative consequences? Samson surely didn't expect it to end this way, but life has a way of doing that to us: we think we have a sure thing and then it falls through. Pray for God to show you choices you are making that will not lead to negative consequences. But if you do make a wrong choice, pray that God shows you the lesson you need to learn from it, so you don't repeat the same mistake again.

Revenge
Judges 15:1-8

Later on, at the time of wheat harvest, Samson took a young goat and went to visit his wife. He said, "I'm going to my wife's room." But her father would not let him go in.

"I was so sure you hated her," he said, "that I gave her to your companion. Isn't her younger sister more attractive? Take her instead."

Samson said to them, "This time I have a right to get even with the Philistines; I will really harm them." So he went out and caught three hundred foxes and tied them tail to tail in pairs. He then fastened a torch to every pair of tails, lit the torches and let the foxes loose in the standing grain of the Philistines. He burned up the shocks and standing grain, together with the vineyards and olive groves.

When the Philistines asked, "Who did this?" they were told, "Samson, the Timnite's son-in-law, because his wife was given to his companion."

So the Philistines went up and burned her and her father to death. Samson said to them, "Since you've acted like this, I swear that I won't stop until I get my revenge on you." He attacked them viciously and slaughtered many of them. Then he went down and stayed in a cave in the rock of Etam.

~ Judges 15:1-8

Previously, we read about Samson's wedding celebration. Samson offered up a riddle to the wedding party for their entertainment with a large price attached to it. The guys were frustrated that they couldn't figure out the answer, so they begged Samson's wife to give them the answer, which she got out of Samson and gave them. Samson got mad at this, and the situation ended with their marriage not being consummated, and the bride's father gave her to one of the groomsmen. Samson, however, apparently thought that they were actually married.

So why did Samson need to go somewhere to visit his wife, if they were married? It was actually fairly common in that society that when the bride and groom were from two different cultures, the bride would primarily live with her family and the groom would regularly visit her. The purpose of staying apart like that was to avoid cultural tensions between the bride and her in-laws, since more often than not the bride would move to where the groom lived. Samson was an Israelite and his bride was a Philistine, so that applies here, and the bride was staying with her Philistine family in Timnah.

It appears that Samson felt guilty for his actions at the wedding, so he brought the young goat as an apology to his bride's family. Samson's intention at this visit was to make things right with his bride's family and to finally consummate the marriage, since he didn't know that her father had already given her away to another man.

Samson technically had legal claim to receiving his bride, so her father offered a sister instead to fulfill his obligation of a bride for Samson. Samson, however, demonstrates his temper once again. He did have some grounds for getting mad, since he should have been able to marry the bride he chose, but he also messed up at the wedding ceremony. But instead of just taking his anger out on the bride's family, Samson's temper escalates, and he takes his anger out on the Philistines as a whole!

Samson's method of revenge destroyed all the crops of the Philistines in that area - grain, grape vines, and olive trees. This is a pretty big deal, because that destruction was quite severe. It's also a big deal because Israelite law explicitly identifies burning crops as a serious offence in Exodus 22:6, for which the person who started the fire must make restitution.

But the hot-tempered Samson was naturally not willing to make restitution for the damage he caused, so the Philistines retaliate. They burn Samson's wife (who was actually another man's wife at this point) and her father to death! The irony here is that back in Judges 14:15, the bridal party threatened this very thing against her if she didn't get the answer to the riddle from Samson. And the retaliation doesn't stop there! Samson gets back at the Philistines for the murders by killing thousands more Philistines.

You may have noticed that things escalated rather quickly here. Samson offers a riddle at the wedding, the men use trickery to answer it, Samson reacts in anger causing his father-in-law to give his bride away, then Samson burns lots of crops, the Philistines murder Samson's bride and father-in-law, and Samson kills thousands more Philistines. Due to tempers and revenge, a small thing of offering a riddle ends up killing thousands of people! Pretty crazy, right?

But that's how sin works. Think about how quickly a little white lie can escalate into much larger deception. You have to tell another lie to cover up for the one you told, and then another, and another. I once saw a play at a local community theater that depicted just that, called "Run for Your Wife." A cab driver has a very carefully planned schedule to spend time with two different wives, and one night he gets caught up with the police because he intervened in a mugging he saw, and the whole situation gets crazy! Lie after lie is told to try and cover up his indiscretion, and the main character even gets neighbors involved in his scheme of lies as well. By the end of the play, there are so many lies that when he finally tells the truth, no one believes him!

Often our sins don't escalate to the nature of killing thousands of people like Samson did, but they can still have a big effect on many people's lives. People can get into legal trouble, they could be injured because of our actions, and relationships are often broken. What may feel like a "no big deal" sin to us can cause serious damage in our lives and the lives of those around us. Remember that when you're faced with the temptation to do something dishonest: resisting the temptation to give in to sin will save us a lot of grief in the future, since no sin stays small.

Complacency
Judges 15:9-13

The Philistines went up and camped in Judah, spreading out near Lehi. The people of Judah asked, "Why have you come to fight us?"
"We have come to take Samson prisoner," they answered, "to do to him as he did to us."
Then three thousand men from Judah went down to the cave in the rock of Etam and said to Samson, "Don't you realize that the Philistines are rulers over us? What have you done to us?"
He answered, "I merely did to them what they did to me."
They said to him, "We've come to tie you up and hand you over to the Philistines."
Samson said, "Swear to me that you won't kill me yourselves."
"Agreed," they answered. "We will only tie you up and hand you over to them. We will not kill you." So they bound him with two new ropes and led him up from the rock.
~ Judges 15:9-13

Samson was in hiding because he had just killed thousands of Philistines. Because of Samson's actions, the Philistine army moved into Judah to keep an eye on what was going on. They figured Samson would be hiding somewhere in Judah, and his fellow countrymen would likely know where. The people of Judah didn't want to fight the Philistine army, so they went to get Samson out of hiding in order to keep the peace.

The Israelites, including the territory of Judah, were being oppressed by the Philistines, but it wasn't as difficult for them as previous occupations had been. Judah had the opportunity here to rise up against the Philistines with Samson as their leader, but they didn't take that opportunity. They wanted to keep the status quo and not rock the boat. They would rather be ruled by the Philistines than rise up against them, even though Samson had clearly shown that he had the capability to lead a rebellion.

The men of Judah would have known that handing Samson over to the Philistines would likely be certain death for him, especially since they were so mad at him for the destruction he had previously caused. But Judah did it anyway! One man's life was evidently worth it to keep the status quo.

Samson didn't want to kill his own countrymen, or have them kill him out of fear, so they agreed to simply tie him up and hand him over. They even used new ropes for added strength so Samson wouldn't break them.

Judah took the easy way out here. They chose complacency over doing what was right. The right thing to do would have been to rise up against the Philistines, who were corrupting Israel with their worship of pagan gods. Israel was not meant to be oppressed by other nations; they were meant to worship the one true God and be led by Him and whatever leader He appointed. But they chose to do nothing rather than fight for what was right.

Where are you complacent in your life? What issues are you not standing up for that you should? We all have times in life when we should take action, but we don't. I encourage you to ask God where you're sinning by not taking action, and to be empowered by His Spirit to do what's right.

Samson's Battle

Judges 15:14-20

As he approached Lehi, the Philistines came toward him shouting.
The Spirit of the Lord came powerfully upon him. The ropes on his
arms became like charred flax, and the bindings dropped from his
hands. Finding a fresh jawbone of a donkey, he grabbed it and
struck down a thousand men.
Then Samson said, "With a donkey's jawbone I have made donkeys
of them. With a donkey's jawbone I have killed a thousand men."
When he finished speaking, he threw away the jawbone; and the
place was called Ramath Lehi.
Because he was very thirsty, he cried out to the Lord, "You have
given your servant this great victory. Must I now die of thirst and fall
into the hands of the uncircumcised?" Then God opened up the
hollow place in Lehi, and water came out of it. When Samson drank,
his strength returned and he revived. So the spring was called En
Hakkore, and it is still there in Lehi.
Samson led Israel for twenty years in the days of the Philistines.
~ Judges 15:14-20

Samson was hiding from the Philistines, and his own countrymen in
Judah found him and turned him over to the Philistine army. Judah
was not willing to fight with Samson to stand up for what was right;
they simply handed him over, likely thinking that Samson would die
at the hand of the Philistines. They had the opportunity to rise up and
potentially dominate over the Philistines, but they didn't.

But Samson didn't die! He was empowered by God's Spirit, and his amazing strength was shown by killing 1000 men with the jawbone of a donkey. While this was an amazing feat, remember that Nazirite vow that Samson had on his life since before he was born? Part of that vow was that he could not have contact with anything dead. The donkey whose jawbone Samson used would have had to have been dead, so Samson was violating that part of his vow again.

After Samson's great victory, he comes up with a poem for his victory chant. His poem does make more sense in the original Hebrew, since the words for donkey ("hamor") and heap or pile ("homer") sound more similar. The carcasses of donkeys were often thrown outside the city wall, which is similar to the disgraceful death that the Philistines received.

In Israelite culture, names are often significant. The place where this happened was originally called Lehi, which means "jawbone," but then it was renamed Ramnath Lehi, which means "jawbone hill." The name change was likely in honor of the "hill" of dead Philistines caused by Samson.

Samson acknowledged God's victory in that battle and didn't take the credit for himself, but he was still physically drained after it. I would imagine that killing 1000 Philistines would be a lot of work, especially with only a donkey's jawbone for a weapon! God provided for Samson's physical needs, just as he had many generations earlier for the Israelites in the wilderness (see Exodus 17:6).

Samson may not have been proclaimed an "official" judge over Israel, but after this incident the people looked to him as their leader for the next 20 years.

Samson allowed God to empower him to victory, while the rest of Judah was still cowering in apathy. They just didn't care about their situation enough to do anything about it.

In your life, are you empowered, or are you apathetic? Do you care about what's going on in the world around you enough to be motivated to do something about it? Or are you just sitting back and letting others rule over you, because you don't care enough to do anything about it? Ask God to empower you with His Spirit like he did with Samson (though that likely doesn't mean for you to kill anyone!). Be empowered instead of living in apathy.

Empowerment
Judges 16:1-3

One day Samson went to Gaza, where he saw a prostitute. He went in to spend the night with her. The people of Gaza were told, "Samson is here!" So they surrounded the place and lay in wait for him all night at the city gate. They made no move during the night, saying, "At dawn we'll kill him."
But Samson lay there only until the middle of the night. Then he got up and took hold of the doors of the city gate, together with the two posts, and tore them loose, bar and all. He lifted them to his shoulders and carried them to the top of the hill that faces Hebron.
~ Judges 16:1-3

At this point in the story of Samson's life, he's been looked to as a leader of Israel for the past 20 years. They respect him for his strength and how God empowered him against the Philistines. Because of how many Philistines he had killed, naturally Samson waited many years before venturing into Philistine territory again. Even in the remote reaches of the Philistines' territory, Samson's reputation was well known.

One of Samson's weaknesses was women. He easily gave into temptation with a prostitute. The Philistine men saw him there, and they decided to wait and see if they could capture him. Even 20 years later, they could not have been happy with all the destruction Samson had caused their people. The men likely fell asleep while they were waiting, but they figured there was no way Samson could get out through the locked city gates overnight anyway.

But, they obviously forgot the amazing physical strength that Samson had shown previously. During the night, Samson goes out and rips loose the large, heavy gates, along with the structure that it was connected to! He doesn't just rip them off and just lay them aside; he carries them away out of the city!

The symbolism of the gates is significant. The city gate was the place where the city's rulers or judges would sit to discuss the issues of the city, similar to a city council that we may have today. Samson showed that even the city's leaders had no power over him.

Samson showed his physical strength and Israel respected him for that, but they should be trusting in God who is even more powerful than Samson. Samson would not have had those powers except through God empowering him. But even with Samson there as evidence of God's power in their lives, Israel still chose to go astray from God and disobey Him.

Today, we have even greater power than Samson! As believers in Jesus, we have the Holy Spirit living in us and empowering us. What are you doing with that power? How are we impacting our culture for God's Kingdom? How are we (figuratively) ripping off the city gates and making an impact? Pray about how God would empower you to make a difference where you live.

Samson Meets Delilah

Judges 16:4-14

Some time later, he fell in love with a woman in the Valley of Sorek whose name was Delilah. The rulers of the Philistines went to her and said, "See if you can lure him into showing you the secret of his great strength and how we can overpower him so we may tie him up and subdue him. Each one of us will give you eleven hundred shekels of silver."

So Delilah said to Samson, "Tell me the secret of your great strength and how you can be tied up and subdued."

Samson answered her, "If anyone ties me with seven fresh bowstrings that have not been dried, I'll become as weak as any other man."

Then the rulers of the Philistines brought her seven fresh bowstrings that had not been dried, and she tied him with them. With men hidden in the room, she called to him, "Samson, the Philistines are upon you!" But he snapped the bowstrings as easily as a piece of string snaps when it comes close to a flame. So the secret of his strength was not discovered.

Then Delilah said to Samson, "You have made a fool of me; you lied to me. Come now, tell me how you can be tied."

He said, "If anyone ties me securely with new ropes that have never been used, I'll become as weak as any other man."

So Delilah took new ropes and tied him with them. Then, with men hidden in the room, she called to him, "Samson, the Philistines are upon you!" But he snapped the ropes off his arms as if they were threads.

Delilah then said to Samson, "All this time you have been making a fool of me and lying to me. Tell me how you can be tied."
He replied, "If you weave the seven braids of my head into the fabric on the loom and tighten it with the pin, I'll become as weak as any other man." So while he was sleeping, Delilah took the seven braids of his head, wove them into the fabric and tightened it with the pin. Again she called to him, "Samson, the Philistines are upon you!" He awoke from his sleep and pulled up the pin and the loom, with the fabric.
~ Judges 16:4-14

We have seen how Samson was a womanizer, and that idea is continued in this passage when Samson falls in love with Delilah. Delilah is from the Valley of Sorek, and interestingly Sorek means "choice wine." Remember that Nazirite vow that Samson had on his life? He was not allowed to have wine or strong drink. Could this perhaps be a foreshadowing of what was to come, that he should not be pursuing a relationship with Delilah? Stay tuned.

We know that Delilah was geographically near Samson since the Valley of Sorek wasn't far away. But with the occupation of the Philistines, the Israelites and Philistines often lived in close proximity, so we do not know from the text whether Delilah was an Israelite or a Philistine. From her close relationship with the Philistine leaders, we can guess that she was likely a Philistine - again, someone Samson should not associate with, simply because he was an Israelite.

In this first story we see about Delilah, she is trying to get Samson to divulge a secret. Does that sound familiar? It should. That's exactly what happened back at his wedding to the woman from Timnah, where his new wife got him to divulge a secret, ultimately causing Samson to lose his wife.

Delilah was promised a fortune for figuring out the secret to Samson's strength. The Philistines didn't want to kill Samson; they just wanted to harness his strength for their side. If you knew a person who had extreme strength, you'd definitely want them to be for you rather than against you, right?

So, Delilah persistently tries to get Samson to reveal his secret. Samson, however, knows what she's up to and 3 times he lies to her and tells her the wrong thing. Each time, of course, she tries it and finds out that he was not truthful with her. Samson is amused by this little game he's playing, but Delilah gets more and more frustrated and agitated with him.

This was not a good foundation for a relationship between Samson and Delilah. Relationships need to be built on trust, and there's no trust when one person is always lying to the other - especially when they're being found out. Samson thought this game of lying to Delilah was amusing, but it would not stay that way. Samson knew better (for now) than to reveal his secret, but he wasn't helping things by giving false information.

Lying will only cause trouble down the road, whether it's with a romantic partner, a friend, or anyone else. Eventually your lies will get found out and you'll be discovered, and the consequences could be major.

What lies have you told, or are you tempted to tell, in your life? Even if you think it's a sure thing that no one will ever find out you lied, first of all that's likely not the case, but more importantly God knows that you've lied. Remember God's natural law and how we'll reap what we sow? That counts for lying, too. At some point, you will have to face the consequences for not telling the truth. Ask the Holy Spirit to empower you to tell the truth in all situations.

Samson Gives In

Judges 16:15-22

Then she said to him, "How can you say, 'I love you,' when you won't confide in me? This is the third time you have made a fool of me and haven't told me the secret of your great strength." With such nagging she prodded him day after day until he was sick to death of it.

So he told her everything. "No razor has ever been used on my head," he said, "because I have been a Nazirite dedicated to God from my mother's womb. If my head were shaved, my strength would leave me, and I would become as weak as any other man."

When Delilah saw that he had told her everything, she sent word to the rulers of the Philistines, "Come back once more; he has told me everything." So the rulers of the Philistines returned with the silver in their hands. After putting him to sleep on her lap, she called for someone to shave off the seven braids of his hair, and so began to subdue him. And his strength left him.

Then she called, "Samson, the Philistines are upon you!"

He awoke from his sleep and thought, "I'll go out as before and shake myself free." But he did not know that the Lord had left him. Then the Philistines seized him, gouged out his eyes and took him down to Gaza. Binding him with bronze shackles, they set him to grinding grain in the prison. But the hair on his head began to grow again after it had been shaved.

~ Judges 16:15-22

Samson has fallen in love with Delilah, and she has been promised a fortune from the Philistine leaders if she can find out the secret to Samson's strength. He's already lied to her about it 3 times, and now she's getting rather frustrated with him.

But Delilah still wants the fortune that was promised to her for revealing the secret, so she keeps it up and keeps nagging Samson about it. This is definitely not a healthy relationship between Samson and Delilah. It obviously is not based on mutual trust and respect, since she's been bribed to betray him, and he keeps lying to her. On top of that, she's nagging him about finding out his secret rather than respecting his privacy on that matter.

Remember what happened back at Samson's wedding to the woman from Timnah? Because of his wife's nagging, he gave in and told the answer to his riddle, causing him to lose a bet. In this situation, the same thing happens. Rather than break off his relationship with Delilah, Samson gives in to her nagging and reveals the true secret to his strength.

From previous chapters, we know that Samson had been careless about 2 of the 3 parts of his Nazirite vow (drinking wine and being around the dead), but it appears that he had been faithful on not cutting his hair. This may have been the most important part of the vow, since the angel who announced Samson's upcoming birth to his parents spoke of it specifically.

Delilah realizes that Samson is finally telling the truth, so she gets the Philistine leaders back and cuts Samson's hair in his sleep. At first Samson thinks all is well when he wakes up, but then he discovers that his strength really has left him, and so has the Lord.

Samson was quickly captured by the Philistines, his eyes were gouged out, and he was imprisoned. Loss of eyesight was considered a terrible curse for Israelites, so this is a very big deal. They gave him the task of grinding grain while imprisoned; grinding grain was usually women's work, so this added to Samson's humiliation. As time went on his hair began to grow back, and the Philistines likely allowed that so they could use his strength for their benefit when it returned.

Samson reaped what he sowed. He was apparently so full of himself and so confident in his abilities that he didn't think he'd lose his strength when his hair was cut, or else his fleshly desires for Delilah got the best of him. Either way, he turned against God, so God turned against him.

Where are you giving in to temptation in your own life? Is there something that you're trying to resist, and you'd be a lot better off if you just walked away from it? Samson would have been better off if he had just walked away from Delilah's temptations, but instead he gave in and reaped what he sowed. What are you sowing in your life that you'll end up reaping the consequences for? Ask God for the strength to turn away and get on His right path for your life.

Samson's Humiliation

Judges 16:23-27

*Now the rulers of the Philistines assembled to offer a great sacrifice
to Dagon their god and to celebrate, saying, "Our god has delivered
Samson, our enemy, into our hands."*
When the people saw him, they praised their god, saying,
*"Our god has delivered our enemy into our hands, the one who laid
waste our land and multiplied our slain."*
*While they were in high spirits, they shouted, "Bring out Samson to
entertain us." So they called Samson out of the prison, and he
performed for them.*
*When they stood him among the pillars, Samson said to the servant
who held his hand, "Put me where I can feel the pillars that support
the temple, so that I may lean against them." Now the temple was
crowded with men and women; all the rulers of the Philistines were
there, and on the roof were about three thousand men and women
watching Samson perform.*
~ Judges 16:23-27

Samson has been captured by the Philistines, thanks to him telling
Delilah the truth about cutting his hair so that he would lose his
strength. The Philistines have gouged out his eyes, imprisoned him,
and humiliated him.

The Philistines attributed their capture of Samson to their god,
Dagon, which is curious since it was clearly Delilah who helped
them. But who is this Dagon?

Dagon was a Philistine idol, and his name means "little fish" or "fish god." He has the body of a fish and the head and hands of a man, sort of like a mer-man. This image is one depiction of Dagon. Dagon was introduced to the Philistines from the Assyrians and Babylonians. The most famous temples of him are at Gaza and at Ashdod (1 Samuel 5:1-7).

Dagon was also noted as being the god of grain. This is pretty significant if you've been following Samson's story. Remember the retaliation and revenge that occurred between Samson and the Philistines in Judges 15:1-8? One of the ways Samson wreaked havoc on the Philistines was to burn their fields of grain. Samson had dishonored Dagon, the grain god, in this act. It's likely that the Philistines would have believed that this angered Dagon, therefore Dagon would have been out to catch Samson as well, which is why they praised Dagon for this capture.

Even though 20 years or so had passed, the Philistines still remembered what Samson did to them. All the things they did to Samson were to further mock and humiliate him. Even this festival was humiliating to Samson, since he was put on display to the 3000+ Philistines in attendance, and because it looked like Samson's God had abandoned him.

At this moment in the story, things are looking pretty bad for Samson. He's completely humiliated and both he and his God are being mocked. It looks like there's no way Samson can be victorious over the Philistines now... or is there? Samson asks a servant to help him so he's near the main pillars of the building, setting the stage for what is to come.

So, what does all this have to do with today? Are you in a situation where perhaps it feels like all is lost? Are things going from bad to worse, with seemingly no way out? It can be hard when we don't see the end of the story just yet. Wherever you're at in life, and whether you realize it or not, God knows how this chapter will end for you. It may be the outcome you want, or it may not be, but that's not what's important; what's important is that God gets the glory.

In Samson's life, God was not yet getting the glory at this moment, and the thousands around him were praising Dagon. While those around you likely don't have a physical idol image that they worship, people are often falling into sin by worshiping things other than God. What is God inviting you to do about that? Near the end of this passage, we see Samson setting the stage for what God is about to do. He wasn't just going to sit idly by and watch all of this Dagon worship; he was ready to do something about it, even if it came at great price. Even when all seems lost, God will still come out victorious, both in Samson's life and in yours.

Samson's Grand Finale

Judges 16:28-31

*Then Samson prayed to the Lord, "Sovereign Lord, remember me.
Please, God, strengthen me just once more, and let me with one blow
get revenge on the Philistines for my two eyes." Then Samson
reached toward the two central pillars on which the temple stood.
Bracing himself against them, his right hand on the one and his left
hand on the other, Samson said, "Let me die with the Philistines!"
Then he pushed with all his might, and down came the temple on the
rulers and all the people in it. Thus he killed many more when he
died than while he lived.*

*Then his brothers and his father's whole family went down to get
him. They brought him back and buried him between Zorah and
Eshtaol in the tomb of Manoah his father. He had led Israel twenty
years.*

~ Judges 16:28-31

In the previous passage, Samson set the stage for what God is about
to do. The Philistines were having a big party to worship their god
Dagon with more than 3000 Philistines in attendance, and Samson
was put on display as their great prize. Samson got in place by the
main pillars of the building, and that's where we pick up the story
here.

As he had done previously, Samson once again called on the Lord
for strength. He wanted to be obedient to God's plan, and at this
point in his humiliation, he likely realized (finally) that following

God's plan was the only way to get out of this. Delilah had cut Samson's hair so that he had lost his strength, but his hair had begun to grow back. Samson likely would not have regained his full strength on his own without God's power back on him.

So, what does Samson do? He brings the roof down - literally! He pushes on the pillars with all of his strength (and help from God), and the whole place comes crashing down, killing all of the dignitaries inside and the 3000 Philistines up on the roof. While Samson had killed many Philistines a few times before, this was his largest slaughter yet. It also came at the greatest price – Samson, too, lost his life that day. Samson would gladly die with the Philistines according to God's plan rather than continue to live a humiliated life among them.

Because of this final act of faith, Samson was considered by the writer of the New Testament book of Hebrews to be a "hero of the faith," in Hebrews 11:32. He is only mentioned very briefly, but he is there. Throughout his life, Samson failed to live up to the standards of the Nazirite vow that was placed on him, but God still used him. Samson was ruined by his own lusts, but God still used him. Samson was an example of great potential of working for God, and even though he did not have true obedience to God or good character, God still used him.

Samson did get revenge on the Philistines, but only in God's timing and using God's methods. He likely would have preferred to kill thousands more of them in some spectacular way where he could live to receive at least part of the glory, but that's not what God had planned. Samson had revealed the secret of his strength to the wrong person (Delilah), so he had to pay the consequences. But God still used Samson to be victorious over the Philistines.

Do you feel unworthy of God using you and your life for His Kingdom? Just look at all the ways Samson messed up, and you shouldn't feel quite so bad. God can and will use anyone for His purposes, and all we need to do is be obedient to Him. Although, like Samson, we will likely still mess up and need God's forgiveness.

133

But if we are willing to be used by God in the method and the timing that He sees fit, He will do miraculous things through us.

What Is a Shrine?

There's a break in the narrative of the book of Judges between chapters 16 and 17, so we'll pause for a few chapters to take a look at some topics that are important for our continued study through this book. For this first topic, we'll look at what shrines are and why they are important.

Based on the simple dictionary definition, a shrine is a type or place of worship. Our English word of "shrine" came either from the Latin "scrinium" meaning a case or chest for books or papers, or the Old French word "escrin" meaning a box or a case. A shrine is dedicated to a specific deity, hero, person, etc. They often contain idols, relics, or other objects associated with the figure being worshiped.

Shrines are often built in a building (like a temple or holy place), or they can be built in houses, yards, etc. They are often constructed at the site of a specific religious event or a holy site. People often make pilgrimages to travel to worship at a particular shrine that has significance to them, many times for religious reasons.

Many religions have shrines, including Christianity, Islam, Hinduism, and Buddhism. In Christianity, Roman Catholics and Eastern Orthodox followers have many shrines. Roman Catholic shrines are often centered on an image of Christ or Mary. They may have statues, paintings, murals, or even mosaics to depict these holy figures. Shrines are often located in alcoves of a church building to be centered on a more individual prayer time. The Eastern Orthodox religion has a strong use of icons, images of Jesus and/or the saints. These icons are often in the front of their worship spaces, depicting various scenes from the life of Jesus. Other forms of Christian shrines are nativity sets or stained-glass windows depicting Biblical figures.

There are also non-religious shrines in our culture today. Remember the Alamo? It's a shrine. War memorials are also examples of shrines, and most towns have them. Findlay, Ohio, where I live, is a town of around 40,000 people, and we have at least two war memorials. There are also Halls of Fame for various sports. I've been to the National Baseball Hall of Fame and Museum in Cooperstown, NY, and the Pro Football Hall of Fame is even closer to home in Canton, OH, though I've never been there. All of these places exist simply to honor people and their achievements.

Shrines definitely do exist today, in various forms. But are they a good thing, or not?

Shrines are good because they honor the memories and accomplishments of those who have gone before us. In the case of war memorials, we have these shrines to show our respect for the sacrifice of those who have fought for our freedom. For sports halls of fame, they exist so we can honor the athletic feats of various sports players. Shrines help us remember the stories of history, whether religious or not. When I attended a Christian grade school, I remember one day our class went into the church building and we studied all of the stained-glass windows and matched them up to the Bible stories they represented. It was a great way to remember each of those stories as I would see the windows after that. Shrines of various sorts can be used as a teaching tool for the younger generations, so we don't forget important stories.

But shrines can also be bad in God's eyes. The main negative aspect of them is the potential for idolatry. If we worship the creation more than the Creator, the shrine or the creation has become our object of worship instead of God, and we're commanded never to do that. Putting anything before God is clearly against His commandments (see Exodus 20:3-6). Many shrines direct our worship to someone or something other than God Himself, and that is a slippery slope.

Just as with anything else in life, it's all about our motivation. Is our motivation for a shrine a way to remember what God has done for us, or is our motivation to worship something other than God? Think about that next time you see something that honors the creation rather than the Creator.

Who, What, and Where Is Ephraim?

There are multiple things named "Ephraim" in the Bible, so in this chapter we'll look at a brief summary of them.

The name Ephraim itself means "I will be doubly fruitful." Its root word is "peri," which means fruit in Hebrew. Add to that a modified form of the "-ayim" dual/double ending and a prefix similar to a very form indicating "I will be," and you end up with the word Ephraim.

The first Ephraim we read about in the Bible is the second son of Joseph (the son of Jacob, with the coat of many colors). We see Ephraim in Genesis 41:52 and 46:20. Ephraim is significant because, like his grandfather Jacob, he received the familial blessing when he should not have. Ephraim's brother Manasseh was older so he should have received the blessing, simply because of birth order. But in Genesis 48:10-14, Joseph's father Israel (aka Jacob) blesses Ephraim first.

The next Ephraim is the tribe of Israel, which was made up of the descendants of Joseph's son Ephraim. The tribes of Israel were mostly formed from Jacob's sons, except for the tribes of Ephraim and Manasseh. These two were from the sons of Joseph, so rather than having one tribe of Joseph (who was Jacob's son), there were two - Ephraim and Manasseh. You might be thinking that there should be 13 tribes then rather than 12, right? Jacob had 12 sons, and if each son became a tribe except Joseph became 2, then that's 13, right? Not quite. Jacob's son Levi became the tribe of the Levites, but since they were priests and served in God's temple, they did not have land, so they were not considered an "official" tribe. The tribe of Ephraim numbered 40,500 people according to the first census in the wilderness after leaving Egypt (Numbers 1:32-33), but only 32,500 when they took the promised land 40 years later, likely due to loss of life during battles.

The tribe of Ephraim's territory in the promised land would later become Samaria in Jesus' day. It was the center of much north-south traffic and was located between the Jordan River and the sea. Ephraim's land was approximately 55 miles by 30 miles, so approximately 1,650 square miles, which is a little larger than the U.S. state of Rhode Island. During the time of the judges, however, Ephraim was haughty, proud, and generally discontent with the other tribes. They felt they had a right to be proud, since the Tabernacle and the Ark of the Covenant (where God's presence dwelled) was in Shiloh in Ephraim for a number of years. Ephraim was knocked off their high horse a bit when those items were removed later on. Ephraim became jealous of the tribe of Judah once Jerusalem in Judah became the capital of Israel.

The term Ephraim also refers to a mountainous area of Israel, Mount Ephraim, and a forest east of the Jordan River. The central district of Palestine was mountainous and occupied by the tribe of Ephraim. This part of the country is referred to in Joshua 17:15 and 19:50. It was densely wooded in Joshua's time, but it also had fertile valleys. Joshua himself was buried there (Judges 2:9). Another significant event in this area of Ephraim was the battle between David and Absalom that was fought there, where Absalom died (2 Samuel 18:6-15).

But wait - there's more! Ephraim was also the name of a gate in the city of Jerusalem. It was on the north side of the city, looking toward the land of the tribe of Ephraim. This gate is referred to in 2 Kings 14:13 and its parallel passage of 2 Chronicles 25:23.

There was also a city called Ephraim in the territory of Ephraim. Jesus went there with his disciples after raising Lazarus from the dead (John 11:54). The town of Ephraim was in the wild hill country north of Jerusalem.

The territory of Ephraim is also the setting for when we pick up Judges 17 in the next chapter, so now you have some background as to who, what, and where that is.

Micah and His Mom

Judges 17

"In those days Israel had no king; everyone did as they saw fit."
~ Judges 17:6

The tone of the book of Judges changes starting in chapter 17. Israel is no longer simply going through the 5-step cycle of sin, slavery, supplication, salvation, and silence. Instead, the nation is continuing a downward spiral into ongoing religious and moral decay, which would lead to Israel wanting a king for their nation.

Here, we're taking a look at Judges 17. Go read the chapter in your Bible before continuing on here. The events in this section of Judges are closely linked and set in the hill country of Ephraim. We meet a man named Micah who we see has stolen 1100 shekels from his own mother. This shows the moral decay that was happening; stealing is bad, but stealing from your own mother is even worse! How much did he steal? Well in that time, a yearly wage was approximately 10 shekels, so this was 110 years of wages! To put that in today's dollars, if we say the average yearly wage is $40,000, then this would be $4.4 million! That's a pretty significant chunk of change.

Naturally, Micah's mother was not happy about this theft, and at first, she didn't know it was her son who stole it, so she cursed the thief. Often curses were pretty effective into scaring the thief to come forward and confess (so they could be un-cursed), and that's exactly what happened here. Micah confesses his crime, and his mother gave him a blessing to undo the effects of the curse.

Micah's mother is grateful, so she desires to dedicate the money back to the Lord. That sounds great, but she doesn't do it quite right. She uses 200 shekels (about 18%) of the money and has a silversmith make an idol with it. God's command to Israel in Deuteronomy 27:15 says, "Cursed is anyone who makes an idol—a thing detestable to the Lord, the work of skilled hands—and sets it up in secret." That seems pretty clear, right? Well Micah's mother violated it on both counts; she made an idol and set it up in secret, in a shrine in their home. Micah and his mom already had a shrine set up in their house, and along with that he made an ephod to wear during their worship of the idol. This is just one episode that demonstrates how everyone did as they saw fit; they felt free to worship whatever they wanted to worship.

In the world of idol worship, there should be a priest for that idol. At first Micah has his son fill that role, until a Levite comes along. Levites were the priestly tribe of Israel, and they had no land of their own but would serve as God's priests throughout Israel. If Levites are already priests for God, then Micah saw this as an upgrade; it's like he has a professional now, not just an amateur! This Levite became a part of Micah's household and was paid a living wage for doing his priestly duties there.

So now, Micah has a shrine, an ephod, and a priest from the tribe of Levi. He figures he's sitting pretty well and will get some great blessings from God for this! But alas, he was sadly mistaken.

Micah tried to do what he thought would please God, but his thinking had gotten so perverted that he really missed the mark. He thought worshiping an idol was what God would want, but that's clearly not how God had commanded the people. Worship is important, and we all worship something, but the key is that we must be worshiping the one true God, not an idol - whether that idol is a physical statue or something else.

Where have you gone astray in your thinking? It can be so easy to do. We may even think we're following Christ when really, we're not. Are you following a Christian teacher and reading their books more than you're following God and reading the Bible? Are you worshiping your church (whether the building, the programs, or the service) rather than God on Sunday mornings?

Just like Micah, we can easily be led astray, even by "churchy" things. Take a look at your life and make sure you're on the right path of truly worshiping God in your everyday life.

Looking for Answers
Judges 18:1-6

In those days Israel had no king.
And in those days the tribe of the Danites was seeking a place of
their own where they might settle, because they had not yet come
into an inheritance among the tribes of Israel. So the Danites sent
five of their leading men from Zorah and Eshtaol to spy out the land
and explore it. These men represented all the Danites. They told
them, "Go, explore the land."
So they entered the hill country of Ephraim and came to the house of
Micah, where they spent the night. When they were near Micah's
house, they recognized the voice of the young Levite; so they turned
in there and asked him, "Who brought you here? What are you
doing in this place? Why are you here?"
He told them what Micah had done for him, and said, "He has hired
me and I am his priest."
Then they said to him, "Please inquire of God to learn whether our
journey will be successful."
The priest answered them, "Go in peace. Your journey has the
Lord's approval."
~ Judges 18:1-6

This passage starts out with the phrase, "In those days Israel had no king." This phrase occurs 4 times in the chapters of Judges 17-21. This shows how much Israel wanted a king to bring the nation back to morality since it had gone so far downhill.

This passage focuses on the tribe of Dan. All of the tribes were supposed to have their own land (except the Levites who served as priests throughout the nation), so why didn't Dan? Back in Judges 1:34-35, the Amorites had confined them to the hill country. They were stuck between the Amorites, Philistines, and their fellow Israelite tribe of Judah. They had land there as given to them by God, but they didn't like to be stuck like that. They wanted something better! This showed their lack of trust in God, that they wanted to have something more than what God had provided for them.

So, the tribe of Dan sent spies to search out a better place for them to live. Those spies ran into the Levite living in Micah's house, who we learned about in the last chapter. The Levite's accent likely caught their attention, since he was from Judea. They were surprised to find a Levite in that area.

The Danite spies assume that this Levite is a priest for the one true God, so they inquire to him about their journey. They had no idea that he was the priest for idol worship. It's likely that the Levite was wearing the ephod while making their request, since ephods were transitioning from use in worship of God to worship of idols. We don't know if the priest's response is really from God or not, but it at least appears favorable for the spies.

This lack of a king in Israel was causing all sorts of unrest and ungodly things to happen. The people of Dan didn't trust God for His provision of their land. The spies didn't know if they were doing the right thing or not. Idol worship was rampant. The spies didn't seem to care whether their answer really came from God or not. If Israel as a nation had been truly focused on God and not entrenched in the immorality of idol worship as well, they would have had clear answers and trust on all of these matters.

Where in your life are you losing focus on God? In Proverbs 3:5-6, we're commanded, "Trust in the Lord with ALL your heart and lean not on your own understanding; in ALL your ways submit to him, and he will make your paths straight" (caps mine). We're not supposed to trust in God with only that part of our lives that attends church on Sunday mornings, but with ALL our heart – that means in ALL areas of our lives. It's so easy to lose focus on God or not be willing to put our trust in Him for everything in our lives, since we like to control things (or try to) ourselves. Look to God for provision in every aspect of your life, and He will provide.

Finding a New Land

Judges 18:7-13

So the five men left and came to Laish, where they saw that the people were living in safety, like the Sidonians, at peace and secure. And since their land lacked nothing, they were prosperous. Also, they lived a long way from the Sidonians and had no relationship with anyone else.
When they returned to Zorah and Eshtaol, their fellow Danites asked them, "How did you find things?"
They answered, "Come on, let's attack them! We have seen the land, and it is very good. Aren't you going to do something? Don't hesitate to go there and take it over. When you get there, you will find an unsuspecting people and a spacious land that God has put into your hands, a land that lacks nothing whatever."
Then six hundred men of the Danites, armed for battle, set out from Zorah and Eshtaol. On their way they set up camp near Kiriath Jearim in Judah. This is why the place west of Kiriath Jearim is called Mahaneh Dan to this day. From there they went on to the hill country of Ephraim and came to Micah's house.
~ Judges 18:7-13

The Israelite tribe of Dan didn't trust God with the land that He had provided for them, so they went looking for different land on their own. The Danite spies had gone 100 miles north, outside the land that God had given to Israel. This new land they found was very secure and very prosperous. It was a long distance from any of their enemies, it had water (springs that formed the source of the Jordan

River), and it had the mountains of Lebanon for protection. It was called Laish, and its residents were basically like sitting ducks here in that spot.

The spies all agreed that they should take this land immediately. So, 600 men set out to conquer this new land, but they did stop for camp first. "Mahaneh Dan" means Dan's camp, and that is evidently how that place was remembered for many years.

The Danite spies said God blessed their taking of this land, but that was likely based on the word from Micah's priest, which really wasn't from God and had nothing to do with taking that land. God had not given this land to Israel, but they wanted to take it for themselves anyway because they liked it. They misinterpreted the priest's word from "God" to fit what they wanted it to say.

Has that happened to you in your life? You see something that is better than what you have, and you want it, whether God is ok with you having it or not. Maybe it's a new car or a new phone that you really want but can't really afford; maybe you would have to give less money to God and His mission to afford this new thing. Do you think God wants you to have that? Do you misinterpret God's Word to justify getting that thing you want?

Honor God by following what He commands you and being content with what He provides for you.

The Fickle Priest

Judges 18:14-21

*Then the five men who had spied out the land of Laish said to their
fellow Danites, "Do you know that one of these houses has an
ephod, some household gods and an image overlaid with silver?
Now you know what to do." So they turned in there and went to the
house of the young Levite at Micah's place and greeted him. The six
hundred Danites, armed for battle, stood at the entrance of the gate.
The five men who had spied out the land went inside and took the
idol, the ephod and the household gods while the priest and the six
hundred armed men stood at the entrance of the gate.*
*When the five men went into Micah's house and took the idol, the
ephod and the household gods, the priest said to them, "What are
you doing?"*
*They answered him, "Be quiet! Don't say a word. Come with us, and
be our father and priest. Isn't it better that you serve a tribe and clan
in Israel as priest rather than just one man's household?" The priest
was very pleased. He took the ephod, the household gods and the
idol and went along with the people.*
~ Judges 18:14-21

The Danite spies had found land they wanted to take for themselves,
and they were about to capture it. They remembered Micah's house,
his shrine, and his ephod. They wanted to make further use of Micah
and his possessions, so they robbed the house of the idol and the
ephod. With 600 against 1 (or maybe a few if you consider the rest

of Micah's household), there wasn't much Micah's priest could do to stop this from happening.

At first the priest was annoyed with the theft, but then he gets invited to join the Danites in their quest. He is easily swayed by the promise of something better, so he gives up on his loyalty to Micah and goes for the better life with higher pay.

This story shows some of the bad things that we as humans do. The priest was fickle in his loyalties and got swept up by whatever good thing came along. That's how he ended up in Micah's house in the first place; Micah gave him an offer that was better than what he had. So, when an apparently better offer came along, the priest took it.

The Danite spies stole from their fellow Israelites without even caring. This behavior was predicted back in Genesis 49:17 which says, "Dan will be a snake by the roadside, a viper along the path, that bites the horse's heels so that its rider tumbles backward." These spies from Dan caused Micah to lose both money and his live-in priest in the theft.

This situation is reminiscent of Psalm 1, where in verse 4 it says, "Not so the wicked! They are like chaff that the wind blows away." The wicked, or those who do not follow God with their lives, will get blown around by the wind. They don't have the solid foundation of faith in God to be their roots, so they are swayed by whatever comes along and appears at the time to be better. This also reflects James 1:6: "But when you ask, you must believe and not doubt, because the one who doubts is like a wave of the sea, blown and tossed by the wind." The context of that passage is about having faith that God will provide what we ask for when we are following Him, but one who doubts and isn't following God will be like a wave in the sea, tossed about by the wind.

A person who stands for nothing falls for anything. Where are you at? Are you standing firm in God's Word and in His plan for your life, even if it's not exactly what you had hoped for? Or are you trying to do things your own way, then hoping that God will bless your decisions? Take a lesson from the people of Dan and Micah's priest, that trusting in God and keeping your loyalty firmly rooted in Him is always the best way.

The Source of Victory
Judges 18:22-31

*When they had gone some distance from Micah's house, the men
who lived near Micah were called together and overtook the
Danites. As they shouted after them, the Danites turned and said to
Micah, "What's the matter with you that you called out your men to
fight?"*
*He replied, "You took the gods I made, and my priest, and went
away. What else do I have? How can you ask, 'What's the matter
with you?'"*
*The Danites answered, "Don't argue with us, or some of the men
may get angry and attack you, and you and your family will lose
your lives." So the Danites went their way, and Micah, seeing that
they were too strong for him, turned around and went back home.
Then they took what Micah had made, and his priest, and went on to
Laish, against a people at peace and secure. They attacked them
with the sword and burned down their city. There was no one to
rescue them because they lived a long way from Sidon and had no
relationship with anyone else. The city was in a valley near Beth
Rehob.*
*The Danites rebuilt the city and settled there. They named it Dan
after their ancestor Dan, who was born to Israel—though the city
used to be called Laish. There the Danites set up for themselves the
idol, and Jonathan son of Gershom, the son of Moses, and his sons
were priests for the tribe of Dan until the time of the captivity of the
land. They continued to use the idol Micah had made, all the time
the house of God was in Shiloh. ~ Judges 18:22-31*

The Israelite tribe of Dan was not happy with the land that God gave them, so they were venturing out to conquer their own land, the territory of Laish. We were introduced to Micah and his idol in Judges 17, and just before this text the Danites had gone to Micah's house and stolen his silver idol.

After the theft, Micah gathers some men who lived near him and they try to go after the Danites to get the idol back. Micah and his small band were able to overtake the Danites since their large numbers, livestock, and children slowed them down more. The Danites pretended not to know why Micah was upset, but really, they were just trying to hide their sin. Any thief should realize that the person they stole from would be upset once they discovered the theft. In this case, Micah is very outnumbered, so he is forced to just give up.

There's an interesting parallel between this story and one about Abram in Genesis 14:10-16. This story takes place shortly after Abram and his nephew Lot had separated from each other, so it's before God's covenant with Abram (and his name change to Abraham), before Abram has any children, and before the destruction of Sodom and Gomorrah for their sinfulness. In this brief story, Lot was captured by the 4 kings of Sodom and Gomorrah. Abram gathers together a very small army, and because God was on his side, Abram's small army overtook the kings and their companies, and they were able to rescue Lot and return the goods that the kings had stolen.

What's the main difference between what's going on with Micah and the Danites, versus Abram and the kings of Sodom and Gomorrah? God. Abram's small army was victorious because he was following the one true God. Micah's small army was defeated and had to give up because they were following his idol, a false god. While the world will always say that larger numbers are better in an army, what really matters is whether that army is following God or a false idol. God is the one who brings victory.

Moving on in this story of the Danites, they were successful in capturing the town of Laish. We saw before that the people of Laish were basically sitting ducks. They were geographically isolated and had no one to help them, so that worked to the Danites' advantage. The way they took over Laish is reminiscent of Abimelech's revenge against Shechem in Judges 9:45-49; it was total destruction. Even though they were worshiping Micah's idol instead of God, they were victorious; but it was at great cost, and they were still disobeying God by taking land that wasn't given to them. Negative consequences don't always come right away, but they will come in God's timing.

The Danites continued to worship Micah's idol instead of the one true God. This would not serve them well in the long run, since worshiping a piece of silver is completely worthless and pointless. The idol didn't have any power to do anything for them, and they showed that it could be easily stolen. God, however, will never leave us nor forsake us, and He is all powerful.

What are you following with your life? Are you following the one true God, who truly can and will take care of you and provide for you? Or are you following something worthless, like Micah's idol? Take a look at your life and see how you spend your time, your money, and your energy, and you'll see what you're really following.

The Levite and His Concubine
Judges 19:1-10

In those days Israel had no king.
Now a Levite who lived in a remote area in the hill country of
Ephraim took a concubine from Bethlehem in Judah. But she was
unfaithful to him. She left him and went back to her parents' home in
Bethlehem, Judah. After she had been there four months, her
husband went to her to persuade her to return. He had with him his
servant and two donkeys. She took him into her parents' home, and
when her father saw him, he gladly welcomed him. His father-in-
law, the woman's father, prevailed on him to stay; so he remained
with him three days, eating and drinking, and sleeping there.
On the fourth day they got up early and he prepared to leave, but the
woman's father said to his son-in-law, "Refresh yourself with
something to eat; then you can go." So the two of them sat down to
eat and drink together. Afterward the woman's father said, "Please
stay tonight and enjoy yourself." And when the man got up to go, his
father-in-law persuaded him, so he stayed there that night. On the
morning of the fifth day, when he rose to go, the woman's father
said, "Refresh yourself. Wait till afternoon!" So the two of them ate
together.
Then when the man, with his concubine and his servant, got up to
leave, his father-in-law, the woman's father, said, "Now look, it's
almost evening. Spend the night here; the day is nearly over. Stay
and enjoy yourself. Early tomorrow morning you can get up and be
on your way home." But, unwilling to stay another night, the man

left and went toward Jebus (that is, Jerusalem), with his two saddled donkeys and his concubine.
~ Judges 19:1-10

As we start Judges 19, we're starting a new story. These last few chapters of Judges (chapters 17-21) contain various stories that show the immorality of Israel. The repetition of the phrase "In those days Israel had no king" (like we see here in verse 1) show that Israel needed a leader to get them back on track with morality.

As with the previous story of Micah and his idol, the characters here are also from the hill country of Ephraim. Here, we see the main characters are a Levite and his concubine. A concubine is similar to a mistress; she's a woman who lives with a man but has lower status than his wife (or wives). This was common in polygamous societies, where a man would have multiple women living with him as wives or concubines. A concubine is sort of a cross between a wife and a slave, so she could not marry her master but was required to live with him as though they were married.

This particular concubine was evidently pretty unhappy with being of the lower concubine status, so she committed adultery with another man. Instead of facing her husband who would have been mad about the situation, she went home to her parents who lived in Bethlehem.

Four months later, the Levite husband wants to get his concubine back, so he goes to her parents' house in Bethlehem to fetch her. The girl's family is happy to see him, since that means their relationship would be restored. The girl's adultery had disgraced her family, so this would be a good restoration.

The father persuades the Levite to stay for a few days, which was the common practice of hospitality back then. Traveling was generally long and difficult, so a few days of rest would be welcomed. So, on the 4th day, and again on the 5th day, the Levite tries to get an early start and go back home, but the father keeps delaying him. The father convinces him to stay for another day each time. We're not told why he didn't want them to leave, so that's left up to the reader's speculation.

Finally, on the 3rd time the father tries to get the Levite to stay, he does get away, but it's much later than planned, which is significant as we will continue on this story in the next chapters. We know the concubine is with him, but we don't know if she went willingly or not.

We see a lot of family interaction going on in this passage. There's the relationship between the Levite and his concubine, the relationship between the concubine and her parents, and the relationship between the Levite and the concubine's father. The story started out with the betrayal of the concubine to her husband, which is obviously a damaged relationship. Then we see that she damages her relationship with her parents as she disgraces them by returning home. Then we see the strained relationship between her father and the Levite because of the continual begging him to stay.

Do you have relationships like this in your life? Are there broken relationships that need mended? Have you done something to disgrace your loved ones? Are you causing someone grief by the way you treat them? Use this story to help you look at your own relationships and where they may be broken and need repair. Ask God to help you see what you are able to mend, and what you need to do better so that strained relationships don't get worse.

Great Expectations
Judges 19:11-21

*When they were near Jebus and the day was almost gone, the
servant said to his master, "Come, let's stop at this city of the
Jebusites and spend the night."*
*His master replied, "No. We won't go into any city whose people are
not Israelites. We will go on to Gibeah." He added, "Come, let's try
to reach Gibeah or Ramah and spend the night in one of those
places." So they went on, and the sun set as they neared Gibeah in
Benjamin. There they stopped to spend the night. They went and sat
in the city square, but no one took them in for the night.*
*That evening an old man from the hill country of Ephraim, who was
living in Gibeah (the inhabitants of the place were Benjamites),
came in from his work in the fields. When he looked and saw the
traveler in the city square, the old man asked, "Where are you
going? Where did you come from?"*
*He answered, "We are on our way from Bethlehem in Judah to a
remote area in the hill country of Ephraim where I live. I have been
to Bethlehem in Judah and now I am going to the house of the Lord.
No one has taken me in for the night. We have both straw and fodder
for our donkeys and bread and wine for ourselves your servants—
me, the woman and the young man with us. We don't need
anything."*
*"You are welcome at my house," the old man said. "Let me supply
whatever you need. Only don't spend the night in the square." So he
took him into his house and fed his donkeys. After they had washed
their feet, they had something to eat and drink.* ~ *Judges 19:11-21*

The Levite's concubine had gone home to her parents, he went to get her, and now they're traveling back to their home. They had gotten a late start thanks to the girl's father, so now they need to stay overnight on their journey.

The city of Jebus was on their way, but it was not an Israelite city, so they likely would not have received good hospitality there and it could have been dangerous for them. It was only 4 more miles to Gibeah, a city belonging to the Israelite tribe of Benjamin, so they continued on there instead. It sounds like these travelers didn't know this, but Gibeah did not have a good reputation; it was known for being very immoral.

In those days you wouldn't just find the local Holiday Inn and check if they had vacancy. Instead, you'd wait in the city square until someone would offer you lodging at their residence. The travelers waited at the city square as was customary, and it was very odd that they were refused hospitality by most of the city.

Finally, an old man offers to help them out. It turns out that he was from the hill country of Ephraim, just as they were. It's always nice to find someone you can connect with when you're away from home. Since this man was not native to Gibeah, he may not have shared the immorality of the town.

Normally, the host would supply all the needs of the travelers who would stay with them, including food. This Levite did not want to be a burden to whoever took them in, so he offered to take care of them, they just needed a place to rest. But the old man still took care of their needs, taking them into his house, providing them with food, and even taking care of their donkeys. He definitely seemed welcoming enough.

Sometimes, our expectations can be different than reality. The Levite and the concubine traveled a little farther just to stay at the Israelite town of Gibeah, rather than take their chances at the non-Israelite town of Jebus. But when they get there, for hours no one is willing to offer them hospitality - and these are their own people! The town they expected to welcome them was in fact unwelcoming to them. It seems like a chance encounter with the old man, but thankfully he does offer to help them. Their expectations were for a restful night in his house, but we'll see how that doesn't happen as we continue on in this story.

Where in your life have you experience a reality that didn't measure up to your expectations? Maybe a friend or family member you expected to help you has let you down, or maybe you have let someone else down.

What are your expectations of God? Do you feel like He has let you down? The reality is that God will never let us down and we can always count on Him, even when His reality may look different than what we expect.

Sodom Revisited
Judges 19:22-30

While they were enjoying themselves, some of the wicked men of the city surrounded the house. Pounding on the door, they shouted to the old man who owned the house, "Bring out the man who came to your house so we can have sex with him."

The owner of the house went outside and said to them, "No, my friends, don't be so vile. Since this man is my guest, don't do this outrageous thing. Look, here is my virgin daughter, and his concubine. I will bring them out to you now, and you can use them and do to them whatever you wish. But as for this man, don't do such an outrageous thing."

But the men would not listen to him. So the man took his concubine and sent her outside to them, and they raped her and abused her throughout the night, and at dawn they let her go. At daybreak the woman went back to the house where her master was staying, fell down at the door and lay there until daylight.

When her master got up in the morning and opened the door of the house and stepped out to continue on his way, there lay his concubine, fallen in the doorway of the house, with her hands on the threshold. He said to her, "Get up; let's go." But there was no answer. Then the man put her on his donkey and set out for home. When he reached home, he took a knife and cut up his concubine, limb by limb, into twelve parts and sent them into all the areas of Israel. Everyone who saw it was saying to one another, "Such a thing has never been seen or done, not since the day the Israelites came up out of Egypt. Just imagine! We must do something! So speak up!" ~ Judges 19:22-30

The Levite and his concubine had been welcomed into an old man's home in Gibeah, which they apparently didn't realize was a very immoral city. They thought that the fact that it was an Israelite city of the tribe of Benjamin meant that they would receive good hospitality there. But, Gibeah had taken on the immorality of the Canaanites and had turned into another Sodom.

These men who came to where the Levite and his concubine were staying were obviously practicing homosexuals. They had seen a new person come into town and thought they could take advantage of that. They were going against God's law, as stated in Leviticus 18:22 and 20:13.

The old man wanted to protect his guest, so instead he offered his daughter and the concubine that came with the Levite. That's exactly what Abraham's nephew Lot did in Sodom (Genesis 19:8), but fortunately in that situation the angels had rescued them.

In that culture, women were considered lowly in society, and molesting a man was considered very disgraceful. The Israelites normally considered raping a woman to be disgraceful as well (as in Genesis 34:7), but it was the lesser of the two evils, so to speak. Promiscuous women were often put to death for their behavior (Deuteronomy 22:21).

We can get an idea here as to why the concubine left the Levite initially, if this was typical of his behavior. She faced abuse all night while he was spared. He knew what was going on and did absolutely nothing to stop it. She survived until dawn, but the abuse was severe enough that by actual sunrise she was dead. The Levite seems especially callous with her, expecting her to be fit for travel that day after what she endured all night.

The corruption that existed in Gibeah was remembered for many generations. It was even written about by the prophet Hosea many years later, in Hosea 9:9 and 10:9. It was not quite as legendary as Sodom and Gomorrah, but it was still very bad and was remembered as such.

This murder was a shock to the nation of Israel, so the Levite does something shocking as well - he cuts up the concubine's body into 12 pieces, and he sends a piece to each of the tribes! To us this may seem especially horrific, but it was his way of showing the people that there was a big problem with immorality right there in their nation, and they need to do something about it. This cutting up was similar to how they would prepare a sacrificial animal (Exodus 29:17, Leviticus 1:6). The tribe of Benjamin, where Gibeah was located, also received one of the body parts.

The purpose of this strange act was to unite the nation of Israel against the evil that was happening within their borders, particularly in Gibeah. It seems like an odd way to do that, but that's what they did.

Israel was obviously becoming more and more immoral. This was the nation that God had chosen, and they were blatantly disregarding His laws! If Israel wasn't following God, then who would? They had adopted morals of other non-God-following peoples, and because of that they had twisted their identity as God's holy people. Much like in today's society, they followed whatever "truth" they wanted to at the moment, rather than constantly following God's absolute truth.

Where in your life have you become immoral and aren't fully following God's law? Immorality can be fun for a time; after all, if sin wasn't fun, we wouldn't do it. But we need to realize that God's natural law is always in effect, and there will always be negative consequences when we don't follow Him.

Unity Through Tragedy
Judges 20:1-11

Then all Israel from Dan to Beersheba and from the land of Gilead came together as one and assembled before the Lord in Mizpah. The leaders of all the people of the tribes of Israel took their places in the assembly of God's people, four hundred thousand men armed with swords. (The Benjamites heard that the Israelites had gone up to Mizpah.) Then the Israelites said, "Tell us how this awful thing happened."

So the Levite, the husband of the murdered woman, said, "I and my concubine came to Gibeah in Benjamin to spend the night. During the night the men of Gibeah came after me and surrounded the house, intending to kill me. They raped my concubine, and she died. I took my concubine, cut her into pieces and sent one piece to each region of Israel's inheritance, because they committed this lewd and outrageous act in Israel. Now, all you Israelites, speak up and tell me what you have decided to do."

All the men rose up together as one, saying, "None of us will go home. No, not one of us will return to his house. But now this is what we'll do to Gibeah: We'll go up against it in the order decided by casting lots. We'll take ten men out of every hundred from all the tribes of Israel, and a hundred from a thousand, and a thousand from ten thousand, to get provisions for the army. Then, when the army arrives at Gibeah in Benjamin, it can give them what they deserve for this outrageous act done in Israel." So all the Israelites got together and united as one against the city.

~ Judges 20:1-11

A Levite's concubine had been killed because of the immorality of the Benjamite city of Gibeah, and now he's doing something about it. He let the entire nation know what happened, so the nation began to unite against the immorality that was taking place in their own nation.

They came together from all areas of the nation and united at Mizpah to plan their course of action. Not quite all of them though - the Benjamites boycotted this gathering, likely since the gathering's purpose was to go against one of their towns.

The Levite tells everyone what had happened to his concubine. He may have exaggerated it a bit to paint himself in a better light, though - after all, he knew what was going on and did nothing to stop it. But he explained why he dismembered his concubine's body and sent them all the pieces, so they would discover what happened and bring attention to it.

Everyone at the gathering agreed that the town of Gibeah needed to be punished for their immorality and wrongful actions. The Israelites united around this cause.

Sometimes it takes a horrible situation to unite a people. In my generation, I experienced September 11, 2001 (I was a sophomore in college then) and saw how our nation united out of the tragedy to step up our game in fighting the war on terror. It was a time of high patriotism and unity in our nation as we were fighting a common enemy. I recall hearing that the Sunday after 9/11/01 had the most church attendance our nation had seen in a long time. For my grandparents' generation, they saw the nation unite against Japan and Germany in World War II. Both of my grandfathers served in WWII, one in the army under General Patton and the other in the navy in the South Pacific. The U.S. got into the war because of the tragedy at Pearl Harbor, and our nation was united in the cause because of the evil we were facing.

Tragedy and loss of life are always sad, but God can (and does) use bad situations to unite a people and to bring about His good (Romans

8:28). The tragedy of the concubine's death united the nation of Israel against immorality so God could bring about His good back into the nation and they would follow Him again.

What has happened in your life that sparked a change? What tragedy has motivated you to change your life to follow God more? If one man's reaction to the death of one woman united an entire nation, what can you do with your one life?

Ready for War
Judges 20:12-18

The tribes of Israel sent messengers throughout the tribe of Benjamin, saying, "What about this awful crime that was committed among you? Now turn those wicked men of Gibeah over to us so that we may put them to death and purge the evil from Israel."
But the Benjamites would not listen to their fellow Israelites. From their towns they came together at Gibeah to fight against the Israelites. At once the Benjamites mobilized twenty-six thousand swordsmen from their towns, in addition to seven hundred able young men from those living in Gibeah. Among all these soldiers there were seven hundred select troops who were left-handed, each of whom could sling a stone at a hair and not miss.
Israel, apart from Benjamin, mustered four hundred thousand swordsmen, all of them fit for battle.
The Israelites went up to Bethel and inquired of God. They said, "Who of us is to go up first to fight against the Benjamites?"
The Lord replied, "Judah shall go first."
~ Judges 20:12-18

Let's review the context of this story. A Levite and his concubine were traveling, and they stopped for the night at Gibeah in the land of Benjamin. While there, the concubine was killed by the sexual immorality of the men of Gibeah. To avenge her death, Israel banded together against the Benjamites and was seeking to get rid of the immorality at Gibeah.

Naturally, the tribe of Benjamin didn't band together with the rest of Israel, because Gibeah was in their territory. But was it right for Israel to fight against their own people? In this circumstance, yes. Deuteronomy 13:5 and 21:21 clearly command Israel that rebellious parts of the nation must be purged: "You must purge the evil from among you." This is similar to the saying about how one bad apple spoils the whole bunch; just one evil town can spread that evil and immorality throughout the entire nation, if it's not taken care of.

The leaders of the tribe of Benjamin could have simply turned over the town of Gibeah to be punished by the nation as a whole, but instead they chose to fight. What began as simply trying to rid the nation of one evil town, now became a civil war. The other 11 tribes were fighting against Benjamin.

In Genesis 49:27, it was predicted that the Benjamites would be good warriors, and this held true. We see in this passage in Judges that they were so good with the bow and slingshot that they could use it with either hand! So, if some of the men from Gibeah were among these skilled fighters, it's understandable that Benjamin would be reluctant to hand them over to be punished and likely killed. So, the rest of Israel came with a huge army of 400,000 men to fight against Benjamin's 26,000 men.

But rather than rushing into battle, Israel inquired of God as to how to proceed. This was a big deal for Israel to be fighting against herself, so fortunately, they did involve God in this matter.

Do you apply this idea in your own life? Do you inquire of God before making big decisions in your life, or even small decisions? Or do you just rush in, thinking you can handle it yourself? Israel's 400,000 men versus Benjamin's 26,000 sounded like good odds for them to just rush in and start fighting, but instead they set a good example for us and turned to God first. They asked God, and then actually listened to and followed His answer. I encourage you to do the same in your life.

Expectations of Victory
Judges 20:19-28

*The next morning the Israelites got up and pitched camp near
Gibeah. The Israelites went out to fight the Benjamites and took up
battle positions against them at Gibeah. The Benjamites came out of
Gibeah and cut down twenty-two thousand Israelites on the
battlefield that day. But the Israelites encouraged one another and
again took up their positions where they had stationed themselves
the first day. The Israelites went up and wept before the Lord until
evening, and they inquired of the Lord. They said, "Shall we go up
again to fight against the Benjamites, our fellow Israelites?"
The Lord answered, "Go up against them."
Then the Israelites drew near to Benjamin the second day. This time,
when the Benjamites came out from Gibeah to oppose them, they cut
down another eighteen thousand Israelites, all of them armed with
swords.*

*Then all the Israelites, the whole army, went up to Bethel, and there
they sat weeping before the Lord. They fasted that day until evening
and presented burnt offerings and fellowship offerings to the Lord.
And the Israelites inquired of the Lord. (In those days the ark of the
covenant of God was there, with Phinehas son of Eleazar, the son of
Aaron, ministering before it.) They asked, "Shall we go up again to
fight against the Benjamites, our fellow Israelites, or not?"
The Lord responded, "Go, for tomorrow I will give them into your
hands."*
~ Judges 20:19-28

The nation of Israel is at war with itself, specifically against the tribe of Benjamin. Israel had 400,000 soldiers up against Benjamin's 26,000. The reason for the war was that the city of Gibeah (in Benjamin) was evil and needed to be taken care of. Israel had asked God how to proceed before rushing into battle, so going in, they were confident of victory.

But on the first day, Benjamin slaughters 22,000 Israelites! Remember that Benjamin had some extremely skilled warriors. But on that day, they killed almost as many Israelite men as Benjamin had in their army.

So, Israel asks God again if they should continue to go against their fellow tribe. God says yes. They want to make sure they're doing the right thing and didn't misinterpret what God told them initially. They were probably second guessing themselves after this initial defeat, but God gives them the assurance that they are to move forward.

On the second day, Benjamin slaughters another 18,000 Israelites! This is less than the first day, but now they've lost a total of 40,000 from their army – a full 10% of what their starting army.

Again, Israel feels defeat instead of the victory they were expecting, so they ask God for further confirmation. This time they also fasted and made sacrifices to show their loyalty, devotion, and commitment to God. Israel was ready to give up, especially since they were fighting against and being killed by their own countrymen. But God assures them that victory is coming.

God was teaching Israel that the victory doesn't depend on the size of the army but on their trust in Him. He wanted them to keep coming to Him and showing their trust and to not give up when things got a little hard.

Have you lived that out in your life? Maybe you expect something to be an easy win, but then it ends up being a lot harder than you expected. Do you give up? Or do you keep turning to God? Are you focused on your preparation and your skills, or are you focused on what God is doing? Victory may not always be ours, but victory is always because of God.

Victory Is God's
Judges 20:29-36

Then Israel set an ambush around Gibeah. They went up against the Benjamites on the third day and took up positions against Gibeah as they had done before. The Benjamites came out to meet them and were drawn away from the city. They began to inflict casualties on the Israelites as before, so that about thirty men fell in the open field and on the roads—the one leading to Bethel and the other to Gibeah. While the Benjamites were saying, "We are defeating them as before," the Israelites were saying, "Let's retreat and draw them away from the city to the roads."

All the men of Israel moved from their places and took up positions at Baal Tamar, and the Israelite ambush charged out of its place on the west of Gibeah. Then ten thousand of Israel's able young men made a frontal attack on Gibeah. The fighting was so heavy that the Benjamites did not realize how near disaster was. The Lord defeated Benjamin before Israel, and on that day the Israelites struck down 25,100 Benjamites, all armed with swords. Then the Benjamites saw that they were beaten.

Now the men of Israel had given way before Benjamin, because they relied on the ambush they had set near Gibeah.

~ Judges 20:29-36

Israel was fighting a battle against their own tribe of Benjamin in order to rid the nation of the immoral town of Gibeah. Even though Israel had a significantly larger army, they suffered defeats on the first two days of battle. They kept seeking God's will, and God kept telling them to continue the fight.

On the third day, Israel finally experienced the victory they had been expecting! The day starts out like the previous two, with Benjamin striking down some of Israel's men. But this time the loss was only 30 men, significantly less than the 40,000 total from the previous two days. Israel then changed their strategy to an ambush.

Benjamin at first thought they were winning again, but the ambush changed everything. There were 26,000 Benjamites, and Israel killed 25,100 of them! After that crushing loss, Benjamin admitted defeat.

It is significant that this is the third day of battle, because three is an important number in the Bible. Jesus rose from the grave on the third day, for example. This third battle would be decisive in the war, and it was.

If Israel hadn't been following what God commanded them, they likely would have lost again. It was clearly the Lord who won the battle, not Israel's strength. They kept seeking God for counsel, and because of that He gave them the victory as He had promised to do. The immoral town of Gibeah was successfully purged from the nation rather than leading them astray.

What are you allowing the Lord to do in your life, rather than doing it yourself? Are you open to hearing a change of strategy from God, or are you too set in your own ways? Following the Lord is what wins the battle, not only in actual war but in every decision of our daily lives.

Natural Law for Benjamin
Judges 20:37-48

Those who had been in ambush made a sudden dash into Gibeah,
spread out and put the whole city to the sword. The Israelites had
arranged with the ambush that they should send up a great cloud of
smoke from the city, and then the Israelites would counterattack.
The Benjamites had begun to inflict casualties on the Israelites
(about thirty), and they said, "We are defeating them as in the first
battle." But when the column of smoke began to rise from the city,
the Benjamites turned and saw the whole city going up in smoke.
Then the Israelites counterattacked, and the Benjamites were
terrified, because they realized that disaster had come on them. So
they fled before the Israelites in the direction of the wilderness, but
they could not escape the battle. And the Israelites who came out of
the towns cut them down there. They surrounded the Benjamites,
chased them and easily overran them in the vicinity of Gibeah on the
east. Eighteen thousand Benjamites fell, all of them valiant fighters.
As they turned and fled toward the wilderness to the rock of
Rimmon, the Israelites cut down five thousand men along the roads.
They kept pressing after the Benjamites as far as Gidom and struck
down two thousand more.
On that day twenty-five thousand Benjamite swordsmen fell, all of
them valiant fighters. But six hundred of them turned and fled into
the wilderness to the rock of Rimmon, where they stayed four
months. The men of Israel went back to Benjamin and put all the
towns to the sword, including the animals and everything else they
found. All the towns they came across they set on fire.
~ Judges 20:37-48

This passage may seem like a bit of a repeat, but this section is essentially a re-telling of the battle that we saw in Judges 20:29-36. This is characteristic in Hebrew writing, so it's not unusual that we see this. The narrator tells the battle story again, but with some more details added in.

We see in this passage that the town of Gibeah was quickly captured and set on fire to notify the rest of the army that it had been taken. The psychological impact of this on the Benjamites was significant. They had lost their key city! This would definitely shake their confidence, especially after victories on the previous two days.

All the Benjamites could do was try and run away, but the sheer numbers of the Israelite army made that impossible. Other Israelites from nearby towns even joined in to help cut off the Benjamites' fleeing. Only a few hundred Benjamites (out of their initial 26,000) survived the battle. As the passage notes, they hid in caves in Rimmon for four months.

Israel then went back to the land of Benjamin and methodically destroyed all of the towns with fire. If one town (Gibeah) was immoral, it was likely that immorality had spread to the other nearby towns. Any bit of immorality left in the land could easily spread, so they wanted to destroy it all.

That may seem like a very mean thing to do, but it was actually God's command. Deuteronomy 13:12-18 says that any city with idolaters was to be burned (people and animals), so that's what they did. Gibeah's immorality was very bad (even to the point of killing a concubine who was just passing through), so their punishment was also very bad.

Negative consequences had finally caught up with them for their evil deeds. Gibeah and the tribe of Benjamin were reaping what they had sown, according to God's natural law.

But this natural law doesn't just apply to the nation of Israel; it applies to us today as well. If we sow evil in our lives, we will reap bad consequences. If we sow good in our lives, we will reap good consequences. If we are living an immoral life, then we will be punished for that in some way, like the Benjamites. But if we seek God and His ways in our lives like Israel did, then we will be rewarded with victory.

The Mess

Judges 21:1-9

The men of Israel had taken an oath at Mizpah: "Not one of us will give his daughter in marriage to a Benjamite."
The people went to Bethel, where they sat before God until evening, raising their voices and weeping bitterly. "Lord, God of Israel," they cried, "why has this happened to Israel? Why should one tribe be missing from Israel today?"
Early the next day the people built an altar and presented burnt offerings and fellowship offerings.
Then the Israelites asked, "Who from all the tribes of Israel has failed to assemble before the Lord?" For they had taken a solemn oath that anyone who failed to assemble before the Lord at Mizpah was to be put to death.
Now the Israelites grieved for the tribe of Benjamin, their fellow Israelites. "Today one tribe is cut off from Israel," they said. "How can we provide wives for those who are left, since we have taken an oath by the Lord not to give them any of our daughters in marriage?" Then they asked, "Which one of the tribes of Israel failed to assemble before the Lord at Mizpah?" They discovered that no one from Jabesh Gilead had come to the camp for the assembly. For when they counted the people, they found that none of the people of Jabesh Gilead were there.
~ Judges 21:1-9

A few years ago, my sister-in-law helped us with some filing and organizing of papers at our house, which we hadn't touched for too many years. Before she started, the filing cabinet and the room were relatively neat and organized. It looked okay on the outside, but we knew that there was a mess of papers inside that needed organized, filed, or thrown away. Something had to be done to fix the problem that we knew existed.

What does that have to do with Israel and the book of Judges? First, some context. The events of Judges 19 led up to a civil war in Israel in Judges 20, where the rest of Israel fought against the tribe of Benjamin in order to rid the nation of the immorality that was going on there. Israel won, and Benjamin's army was essentially wiped out. Many of their cities were burned to the ground, including Gibeah, where all of this drama had started.

The Israelites were remorseful over what had happened, and they wept before God at the near total loss of one of their own tribes. It's hard to say whether they realized that their punishment went further than they originally intended, or whether they were just sorry it had to come to this, and that Benjamin deserved such punishment. Either way, they were very remorseful before God that this situation had occurred.

Back in Judges 20:1-2 when Israel assembled at Mizpah before beginning the war, they took the oath against their daughters marrying into the tribe of Benjamin, because of the immorality that was evident in that tribe. Essentially, the men of Benjamin had become like the Canaanites they lived near. Now, however, they were regretting that oath, because it looked like the entire tribe of Benjamin could die out.

But there was an even more important oath, referenced in Judges 21:5: "Then the Israelites asked, 'Who from all the tribes of Israel has failed to assemble before the Lord?' For they had taken a solemn oath that anyone who failed to assemble before the Lord at Mizpah was to be put to death." Who was guilty of breaking this oath? The city of Jabesh Gilead, in the tribe of Manasseh.

Israel was really not in a good state at this time. They had just fought among themselves in a civil war, and now it looked like one tribe would be completely wiped out. On top of that, one city may need to be put to death, simply for not showing up!

All of their oaths seemed to keep getting them in trouble. Israel had to punish the tribe of Benjamin for their immorality, but that punishment left a bigger wound than they had expected. Did they go too far? They did keep checking with God and He kept telling them to move forward, so it appears as though they followed God's direction. But now, their oaths are seeming to get them into more trouble.

So, back to our filing cabinet. In order for my sister-in-law to organize all the paperwork, first it had to all come out and the room turned into what looked like a big mess! There were piles of papers everywhere plus some mess from the paper shredder, since it seems there's no way to empty one of those and not make at least a little mess. The file cabinet had to be emptied before all the papers could be organized and re-filed.

Israel was in that "mess" stage here. They knew there was a problem so they fixed it, but the solution at this point still looked like a huge mess! They haven't gotten to the "neat and organized" part yet.

What in your life feels like you're in the "mess" stage? Do you have a situation that you're working through that seems to be going from bad to worse? Keep trusting God and keep working on what He is calling you to do, and you will keep moving toward the "neat and organized" phase when you're following His will.

Two Problems
Judges 21:10-18

So the assembly sent twelve thousand fighting men with instructions to go to Jabesh Gilead and put to the sword those living there, including the women and children. "This is what you are to do," they said. "Kill every male and every woman who is not a virgin." They found among the people living in Jabesh Gilead four hundred young women who had never slept with a man, and they took them to the camp at Shiloh in Canaan.

Then the whole assembly sent an offer of peace to the Benjamites at the rock of Rimmon. So the Benjamites returned at that time and were given the women of Jabesh Gilead who had been spared. But there were not enough for all of them.

The people grieved for Benjamin, because the Lord had made a gap in the tribes of Israel. And the elders of the assembly said, "With the women of Benjamin destroyed, how shall we provide wives for the men who are left? The Benjamite survivors must have heirs," they said, "so that a tribe of Israel will not be wiped out. We can't give them our daughters as wives, since we Israelites have taken this oath: 'Cursed be anyone who gives a wife to a Benjamite.'"

~ Judges 21:10-18

Israel has two problems right now. First, the tribe of Benjamin is basically going to die out, after they got almost completely wiped out during the civil war in Israel. Second, the city of Jabesh Gilead in the territory of Manasseh didn't show up to the initial meeting, so according to the oath made among Israel, they need to be put to death. In addition, the men from the tribe of Benjamin who remained had been hiding in the caves of Rimmon, so Israel needed to do something to let them know it was alright to come out, and so they could begin to repopulate their tribe.

Israel came up with a creative idea to solve both problems at once: keep the virgins of Jabesh Gilead and give them to the men of Benjamin!

This was a good solution, because of the genealogy of the tribes of Benjamin and Manasseh. Jacob was the father of the nation of Israel, and he had two wives and two servants whom he had children with. One of his wives, Rachel, gave birth to two sons – Joseph and Benjamin. Joseph had two sons, Ephraim and Manasseh. So, Benjamin and Manasseh were uncle and nephew, and therefore closely related in the bloodlines of the nation as they came from the same wife of Jacob.

But what about that whole idea of re-populating a tribe using virgins? Didn't the virgins get a say in the matter? Not really, unfortunately; but their other choice was to die. According to Numbers 31:17-18, the law says it's encouraged to save the virgins (and only the virgins) after a war.

After 4 months of hiding in caves, the remaining men of Benjamin were eager to get out and get on with their lives. However, as it turned out, there weren't enough virgins for the men, and it would not have been right for some of the few survivors to not continue their family lines. Benjamin was already a small enough tribe after having most of their people wiped out!

In verse 15, it says, "The people grieved for Benjamin, because the Lord had made a gap in the tribes of Israel." The word there for "gap" literally means a breach, like a break in a wall. This suggests that Israel really wasn't whole or complete without Benjamin. At this point it seemed like the breach was only partially repairable, given the oaths that had been made previously. Fortunately, Israel comes up with an even better plan, which we'll take a look at in the next section.

What do you feel is broken in your life? Is there a hole that you feel can't be filled? Perhaps you've experienced the death of a loved one, a divorce, a child moving away, a breakup of a relationship or close friendship, etc. We all have places in our life where we feel things aren't quite as they should be and are broken.

What can we do about the holes in our life? Often, we can do nothing to fix them on our own, but God can fill them. He can fill us with His presence and give us His peace about the broken situation, and He likely has a solution for you, even if it may not be what you expect. It won't be the same as what was lost, but just as God will provide a solution for Israel, we, too, can trust in God's perfect timing and will for our lives. We need to trust that He will take care of us and give Him glory in all situations, including the broken ones.

The Loophole
Judges 21:19-24

"But look, there is the annual festival of the Lord in Shiloh, which lies north of Bethel, east of the road that goes from Bethel to Shechem, and south of Lebonah."
So they instructed the Benjamites, saying, "Go and hide in the vineyards and watch. When the young women of Shiloh come out to join in the dancing, rush from the vineyards and each of you seize one of them to be your wife. Then return to the land of Benjamin. When their fathers or brothers complain to us, we will say to them, 'Do us the favor of helping them, because we did not get wives for them during the war. You will not be guilty of breaking your oath because you did not give your daughters to them.'"
So that is what the Benjamites did. While the young women were dancing, each man caught one and carried her off to be his wife. Then they returned to their inheritance and rebuilt the towns and settled in them.
At that time the Israelites left that place and went home to their tribes and clans, each to his own inheritance.
~ Judges 21:19-24

Israel had a dilemma. The tribe of Benjamin had been nearly wiped out by the civil war in Israel, and they thought they had solved two problems at once by giving the virgins from Jabesh Gilead to the remaining men of Benjamin to repopulate, but there weren't enough women to go around. So, Israel had to get a bit creative in how to address this.

183

The oath that Israel had taken before the war (referenced in Judges 21:1) said that the other tribes could not GIVE their daughters to Benjamin in marriage. But if Benjamin STOLE their daughters, that wouldn't be breaking their oath, right?

There was a festival coming up in Shiloh, and many people would be gathered there. This celebration is likely along with the celebration of the Passover, as the dancing may be an imitation of Miriam's dancing in Exodus 15:20-21.

The men of Benjamin were given very detailed instructions on where they were to go, primarily because they would not have been familiar with the hill country of Ephraim. This instruction would help them make a quick escape, should it become necessary. It's especially interesting that the Benjamite men were essentially told to ambush the young women; this is the same technique that Israel used to defeat Benjamin in the war, and now it would be used to build their tribe back up.

This method was very unorthodox, and it would likely make the family members mad that their girls were essentially stolen from them. Marriages were usually arranged by the father, so this was contrary to their customs. But, the leaders of Israel would support the men of Benjamin in this, in case the families got mad over the action. They needed to fill the gap left by the tribe of Benjamin, and the women of Jabesh Gilead weren't enough so they needed more. They technically aren't breaking the oath since they're not "giving" the girls to them.

After this plan was put into action, Israel had now taken care of the issues with Benjamin, and the army could disband. However, this episode was one of the most tragic in Israel's history due to the great loss of life in the war and the fact that they were fighting among themselves rather than against an enemy nation.

But what about Israel's actions to get around their oath – were they acceptable? This issue is often referred to as the letter of the law versus the spirit of the law. They were following the letter of the law in that they technically didn't break it by not giving their daughters in marriage. But, the spirit of the law is about the heart's attitude. Israel was trying to find a loophole to get around what they promised.

This reminds me of something my brother and I did when we were little. It was nap time, but we were getting toward the age of being too old for naps, so Mom told us to stay in our rooms. Well, our bedroom doors were right next to each other in the one corner of the hallway. There was different carpeting in the hallway than our bedrooms, so there was a clear line of what "in our rooms" meant. So, he sat in the doorway at the edge of his room and I sat in the doorway at the edge of mine, and we put a board game on the floor of the hallway and played it.

Did my brother and I follow the letter of the law? Yes; we were technically both in our own bedrooms. However, we were not following the spirit of the law, which was that we were to be by ourselves napping, or at least being quiet separately in our own rooms, not interacting.

Israel followed the letter of their oath by technically not "giving" their daughters in marriage, but they disobeyed the spirit of their oath by coming up with a loophole to get around it. They did need to fill the gap in the tribe of Benjamin, but they would have been much better off if they simply hadn't made the oath in the first place.

Where in your life are you following the letter of the law, but breaking the spirit of the law? Maybe you're "just friends" with that person, but in your heart, you're wishing it was more and therefore not being true to your spouse in your heart. Maybe you're reading your Bible every day because you feel you're supposed to, but your heart really isn't in it and you aren't doing it to draw closer to God. Take a look at your life and see where your motivation may not be what God would desire, even if your actions appear okay.

Conclusion

Judges 21:25

"In those days Israel had no king; everyone did as they saw fit."
~ Judges 21:25

The very last verse of the book of Judges, quoted above, sums up the entire story pretty well.

This time in Israel was a period of unrest and anarchy. The people were often without a leader between each of the judges that God provided, so at those times they lived in idolatry and immorality. Sin was prominent, both individually and on a national level, so God repeatedly allowed punishment to come on them as they would get attacked or captured by their enemies.

There is a 5-step pattern that we see Israel repeating multiple times throughout the book Judges. The pattern is this:
1. Sin - The people disobey God.
2. Slavery - God allows them to be enslaved by their enemies.
3. Supplication - The people cry out to God for deliverance.
4. Salvation - God delivers them.
5. Silence - There is a time of peace.

We saw this pattern repeated many times throughout the book, and it really is the natural cycle of human life. We mess up in some way, God gives us a consequence for that according to His natural law, we realize we messed up and cry out to God for forgiveness, God forgives us, and we have a time of peace before we start the cycle all over again by messing up. They did what they thought was right, which often didn't line up with what God wanted them to do.

We look back at Israel in the book of Judges and often think, "How stupid were they, that they didn't learn already?!" But we need to remember that they would go through this cycle over the course of decades or generations, not just in a few days or months. Every generation needed to experience it in order to learn from it. If we take an honest look at our own lives, we've probably gone through this same cycle more times than we'd like to admit.

But, God is good! He loves His people and continually works at bringing them back to Himself. Punishment may not feel like a good thing, but it is necessary in Israel's lives and in ours to bring us back when we go astray and disobey Him.

So, what have I learned from this study through the book of Judges?

Even with many years of Christian education and a seminary degree, I had never done this detailed of a reading or study through the book of Judges. I had studied many parts of it before, but never the entire thing like this. I learned many details to the stories that I had never realized before, and I read some stories in the book that I don't believe I had ever read previously.

I also learned about the other nations surrounding Israel and their interactions. I studied a number of different people groups from that time period that I really didn't know much about prior to this study.

By far the biggest truth I learned from this study on Judges was that you will reap what you sow! If you turn away from God and disobey Him, eventually He will let you get punished for that choice. But when we turn back to God, He is always there welcoming us back.

My religion class teacher from 9th grade summed up this theory well: "O=B and D=C." That stands for Obey = Blessed and Disobey = Cursed, which is God's natural law in a nutshell. When we obey Him, we will be blessed. When we disobey Him, we will be cursed.

This is what Israel needed to keep learning and re-learning throughout the book of Judges, and we need to keep learning and re-learning this in our own lives as well.

Thank you for joining me on this journey through Judges. I pray that you have been blessed through it, and this book of stories from so many years ago has influenced your life today and helped you to draw nearer to the good God who created all of us.

About the Author

Katie Erickson is a native of Dearborn, Michigan. She migrated to Ohio to earn her bachelor's degree in electrical engineering from Ohio Northern University in 2003 and has lived in northwest Ohio ever since. A lifelong Christian, Katie was called to seminary and began her studies at Winebrenner Theological Seminary in 2007, earning her Master of Divinity degree in 2010 with a specialization in the Biblical languages of Greek and Hebrew. She has a passion for digging into the original languages of the Bible to interpret them more accurately, both for personal spiritual growth and to help others in their understanding of the Scriptures.

Katie continues to work in the engineering field, as an electrical design engineer for Ridge & Associates, Inc. in Findlay, Ohio. Aside from her engineering job, Katie has been writing weekly blog posts for Worldview Warriors and has been appearing monthly on the Do Not Keep Silent radio show since 2011. She has taught Biblical Hebrew in a few different contexts, has spoken at a variety of events, and regularly provides pulpit supply services to various churches whenever there is a need. Katie has a passion and skill for editing, assisting authors in self-publishing their works, and graphic design. Her other interests include crocheting, knitting, anything to do with technology and gadgets, and enjoying her pet cats, frogs, and bearded dragons.

Equipping Students to Impact This Generation
For Jesus Christ

www.WorldviewWarriors.org

Worldview Warriors
P.O. Box 681
Findlay, OH 45839

info@worldviewwarriors.org
(419) 835-2777

We provide free weekly resources available to use in
personal study, small groups, Sunday school classes, sermons, etc.

Contact us to book Katie Erickson or one of our other speakers
for interviews or your next event!

Find us on Facebook
www.Facebook.com/WorldviewWarriors

DONOTKEEPSILENT

Speaking out the name of Jesus Christ in action and in word

DO NOT KEEP SILENT

We are a talk radio show that plays great music as well for those
wanting to grow in their relationship with Christ

90.1 FM - WXML in Upper Sandusky, OH area
Sunday evenings from 7pm - 9pm

Radio4Him online
Wednesday evenings from 7pm - 9pm

We have a 2-hour program and a 30-minute program available

DoNotKeepSilent.com

Facebook.com/DoNotKeepSilent

Check out other books from

WORLDVIEW WARRIORS
PUBLISHING

Tough Questions:
Biblical Answers to Life's Challenges
By Katie Erickson

What the Bible Says About...
By Katie Erickson

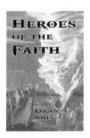

Heroes of the Faith
By Logan Ames

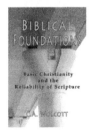

Biblical Foundations:
Basic Christianity and the Reliability
of Scripture
By C.A. Wolcott

Find them all at WorldviewWarriors.org!